ASTROLOGICAL MARKERS OF ADD AND ADHD

by
Gayle Geffner

ACS Publications
an imprint of Starcrafts LLC

Astrological Markers of ADD and ADHD

Copyright © 2014 by Gayle Geffner
All rights reserved.

No part of this book may be reproduced or used in any form or by any means—graphic, electronic or mechanical, including photocopying, mimeographing, recording, taping or information storage and retrieval systems—without written permission from the publisher.
A reviewer may quote brief passages.

by Gayle Geffner

Cover and book design by Maria Kay Simms

International Standard Book Number: 978-1-934976-55-5

Published by ACS Publications,
an imprint of Starcrafts LLC
334-A Calef Highway, Epping, NH 03042
http://www.starcraftspublishing.com
http://www.astrocom.com
http://www.acspublications.com

Printed in the United States of America

Dedication

As always, this book is for
my husband,
James,
and my good friends,
Cindy and Danny

Acknowledgments

Thank you to Maria Simms for her expertise in editing, as well as all of her very helpful suggestions and support.

Thank you to Thomas Canfield and Simonne Murphy for aide in my research on Eris and Ceres.

Thank you to Rique Pottenger for programming Asteroid 944 Hidalgo into ACS systems.

A very special thank you to my good friend Lynn Koiner for her help with my research on Ceres, Eris and Saturn. I attended Lynn's lecture at the NCGR 2013 Education Conference in Philadelphia, PA. She presented a lecture, "Medical Astrology and the Frontal Lobe of the Brain." She concludes that the Prefreontal Cortex of the brain (Saturn) is associated with ADD and ADHD. Although we worked independently prior to the conference, we both found Saturn's influence on ADD/ADHD. My research links Saturn karmically to ADD/ADHD. If you get a chance, do not miss Lynn's lecture. Her help with additional research information was incredibly valuable to me.

Table of Contents

Introduction 1
    Phobias and Physical Maladies 1

Chapter 1 THE TELL 4

Chapter 2
PLANETS, NODES, HOUSES and HIDALGO 15
    The Significance of Nodes, Retrogrades and Hidalgo 15
    DEFINITIONS—HOUSES 17
        First House 17
        Second House through Seventh House 18
        Eighth House through Eleventh House 19
        Twelfth House 20
    THE PLANETS 20
        Sun, Moon, Mercury, Mercury Retrograde 20
        Venus, Venus Retrograde, Mars, Mars Retrograde 21
        Jupiter, Jupiter Retrograde 22
        Saturn and the Outer Planets 22
        Saturn Retrograde, Uranus 23
        Uranus Retrograde, Neptune 24
        Neptune Retrograde, Pluto, Pluto Retrograde, Ceres . 25
        Eris, Asteroid 944 Hidalgo 26
    THE ASTROLOGICAL SIGNS 27
        Aries, Taurus 27
        Gemini, Cancer, Leo, Virgo, Libra, Scorpio 28
        Sagittarius, Capricorn, Aquarius, Pisces 29

Chapter 3
ADD/ADHD PLACEMENTS IN INDIVIDUAL CHARTS 30
    EVAN 30
    DARIUS 37
    BETTY 43
    CARRIE 48
    DECLAN 51
    NATHANIEL 57

Chapter 4
THREE CELEBRITIES WITH ADD/ADHD 63
STEVEN TYLER. 63
      Now the ADD/ADHD 64
      An Interesting Midpoint. 68
MICHAEL PHELPS. 68
HOWIE MANDEL. 73
Summary 79

BIBLIOGRAPHY. 80
HIDALGO EPHEMERIS TABLES 81
ABOUT THE AUTHOR 96

Chart Illustrations
Hidalgo. 7
Execution of Hidalgo 13
Evan 31
Darius 39
Betty 45
Carrie. 49
Declan. 53
Nathaniel 59
Steven Tyler. 65
Michael Phelps. 71
Howie Mandel 75

INTRODUCTION

Phobias and Physical Maladies

A phobia, is based on past life events. Perhaps at one time you fell a great distance and are now afraid of heights. Perhaps you drowned and are now afraid of water. Natal astrology charts bear this out. An actual physical malady is created by a fear so strong that it is no longer mental or a phobia (definition of phobia—unreasonable fear), but manifests itself on a far deeper level. It manifests as a malady in your actual physical being which is a medical, diagnosable condition. This diagnosable condition was caused by even greater trauma (or at least a trauma to which you reacted more strongly) and in the case of ADD/ADHD, one that has its roots in humane activity. It appears, astrologically, that a person with ADD or ADHD, was a martyr who fought for a humanitarian purpose that may have been a prominent cause of his/her generation. This person may have been persecuted and was martyred for this cause. The astrological indicator in each and every case that I have studied for this book is Asteroid 944, Hidalgo. This Asteroid, combined with other factors in the natal chart, appears to be a strong indicator of ADD and ADHD. That is not to say that everyone with certain placements will have the condition, but it does show in placements of those who do have

ADD and ADHD, just as not everyone with placements of a serial killer will be a serial killer. Asteroid 944 Hidaglo is, however, a place to look for help in learning to identify and cope with ADD/ADHD. I will demonstrate the placements with many examples in the next chapters.

  For someone of my age, ADD and ADHD was not diagnosed as ADD or ADHD until I was a young adult. There was a diagnosis as early as around 1900, but it was not called ADD/ADHD and it was somewhat ignored. I went to school with several children whom I am convinced suffered from ADD or ADHD. They were treated as difficult at best, and often suffered some type of discipline each day. They did not know why they could not concentrate nor why they could not act like the other children. They felt picked upon. I know of one person, whom I used as an example in this book, who actually saw his school records in the principal's office and read about himself, "Unable to learn but does not cause trouble, so pass him along." Can you imagine how this would make a child feel? I wonder how many people would have had better lives and been able to do more with their lives as adults, if they had knowledge of ADD and ADHD at a younger age; and even moreso, the knowledge as to how they could have some control over it, even without current medications. By the way, the person whom I just mentioned who had seen his school records when he was a child, now has a Ph.D. in education!

  The purpose of this book is to explore astrological markers of ADD and ADHD, to give experienced astrologers a heads up on ways to work with each individual astrological chart of people who have either ADD or ADHD. It will also give the new astrologer insight into astrological counseling of those who have ADD or ADHD. Although a new astrologer may not yet be advanced in all methods, I do feel that with increased knowledge of astrology, he or she will find this book useful.

THIS BOOK IS NOT INTENDED TO BE A GUIDE ABOUT WHETHER TO MEDICATE OR NOT, NOR IS IT ABOUT A DIAGNOSIS OF ANY KIND. IF YOU HAVE A CLIENT WHOM YOU THINK APPEARS TO HAVE ADD OR ADHD, THEN

THAT CLIENT SHOULD BE REFERRED TO A PHYSICIAN, IF HE OR SHE IS NOT ALREADY BEING SEEN BY ONE.

This book is intended to be an aid in helping you and your client better to understand why he or she has ADD or ADHD, and then to deal more intelligently and effectively with his or her reaction to it. Astrology can also help one to understand times to work toward overcoming, evolving and learning to cope. In fact, I have found that ADD/ADHD persons tend to be very intelligent. They will appreciate the information set forth in this book. They may take the most simple idea and incorporate it into their everyday lives in order to grow.

CHAPTER 1
THE TELL

When one plays poker each and every player has a "tell." This is something players do that can tip you off as to whether they are bluffing. When it comes to ADD/ADHD, the tell is Asteroid Number 944 Hidalgo. This is why!

When I began looking at the charts of a father and son who have ADD (attention deficit disorder) and/or ADHD (attention deficit hyperactivity disorder), I thought I would see difficult aspects to Mercury and perhaps with hyperactivity, difficult aspects to Uranus or something to do with Gemini. I was somewhat off base in not including all outer planets with this theory. Of all the planets, Saturn plays a large part along with Uranus, the Ascendant, possibly Neptune, and Pluto, and the Nodes. However, the most surprising find was the role of Asteroid No. 944, Hidalgo.

I have known quite a few people with ADD or ADHD, and it seems that ADD and ADHD are more common in males than females. When ADD was finally diagnosed, Ritalin was first used to help with ADD or in most instances hyperactivity, and many educators were against it because of its side effects which are the same as those associated with today's Concerta and Adderal.

Adderal is a central nervous system stimulant that affects chemicals in the brain and the nerves that contribute to hyperactivity and impulse control. Ritilan has the same side effects as Adderal. ADD and ADHD are caused by neurobiologic factors and genetics. One problem with drugs used to treat ADD/ADHD is dependency and sometimes abuse. Other problems are dizziness, nervousness, hypertension, and anyone with heart problems or previous drug abuse problems cannot take them. The same is true of those diagnosed with glaucoma or Tourettes syndrome, and no one under six years is supposed to take them. One important factor is that the prescription medicines work to calm those with ADD/ADHD, but act as speed if they are not needed for one of those conditions. There are homeopathic treatments such as Focus Formula.

I am not medically trained and do not recommend any of the above treatments. This is just background information as to how these problems are treated today. In speaking with people who have ADD/ADHD, I've been told that prescription medications gave them a life they could never have had otherwise. This is not to say that homeopathic medicine would not work over time; I just do not know, and it may not work for everyone. **This book should NOT be used as any type of medical advice.**

There are a group of symptoms suggesting ADD/ADHD that affect concentration and they appear over months. You do not just wake up one day with ADD/ADHD.

According to "Living and Coping with ADHD" by Gayle L. Zieman, Ph.D. in *Parenting New Mexico*, June-July 1999, one way to cope is to carry items that relieve hyperactivity, such as something to fiddle with or a small soft ball to squeeze off and on. Distractions can be reduced by going into a quiet room to read. White noise also helps. Teachers have found that a traditional classroom rather than sitting in a circle also helps with concentration.

Hyperactivity may be suggested when a person never finishes a task. Perhaps a hyperactive person is talking with others and long after the conversation has shifted, begins again talking about the old subject. I know of one person with ADD who may pick up a book or magazine and begin reading when talking to others. Hyperactivity is a little more apparent than just ADD.

If you feel you have or someone you know may have ADD/ADHD, you or this person should see a medical doctor. This book is just describing the astrological markers that may indicate ADD/ADHD.

Now back to the tell, Hidalgo, himself. In order to understand why **Asteroid 944 Hidalgo** plays a large part in natal charts of those with ADD/ADHD, you must understand and really get a feel for the Asteroid. Hidalgo ties in with Saturn, ruler of Capricorn. It is a Centaur-like asteroid. A Centaur is a minor planet with an unstable orbit that is half asteroid and half comet. Some astronomers consider it a defunct comet, no longer having a tail. For the purposes of this book, Hidalgo's orbit is important. At aphelion it is in Saturn's orbit. It does not cross Saturn, but is associated with Saturn's family of comets. It was first discovered in 1920.

According to Zane B. Stein in "The Challenge of Hidalgo," circa 1981, there are two possible sources for Hidalgo's name. The first is from the Spanish *hijo de algo*. In literal translation from Spanish to English, *hijo* is the son of something (*algo*). Hidalgo, then, would be a contraction—not two people. It was associated with lesser nobility in Spain. The father was not great nobility. He was lesser nobility, but still important.

As I discuss the life of Miguel Hidalgo Y Costilla, you can see how this ties in. The Mexican government asked that Asteroid 944 be named Hidalgo after him. His chart is on page 7.

A modern example of lesser nobility would be the poorest kid in the rich kid neighborhood. Those of us who were raised in average homes would look at this person as lucky. We probably had to work for our first car. One person I knew, who was indeed the less wealthy kid in a rich kid neighborhood, had a new Chevy Malibu (a great first car for my generation) for college. His peers had new Corvettes and in his environment this was difficult. His car was less than that of his peers. Everyone in my neighborhood worked for their first car and we were proud. He felt inferior which was laughable from my standpoint but understandable from his. This suggests feelings of lesser nobility.

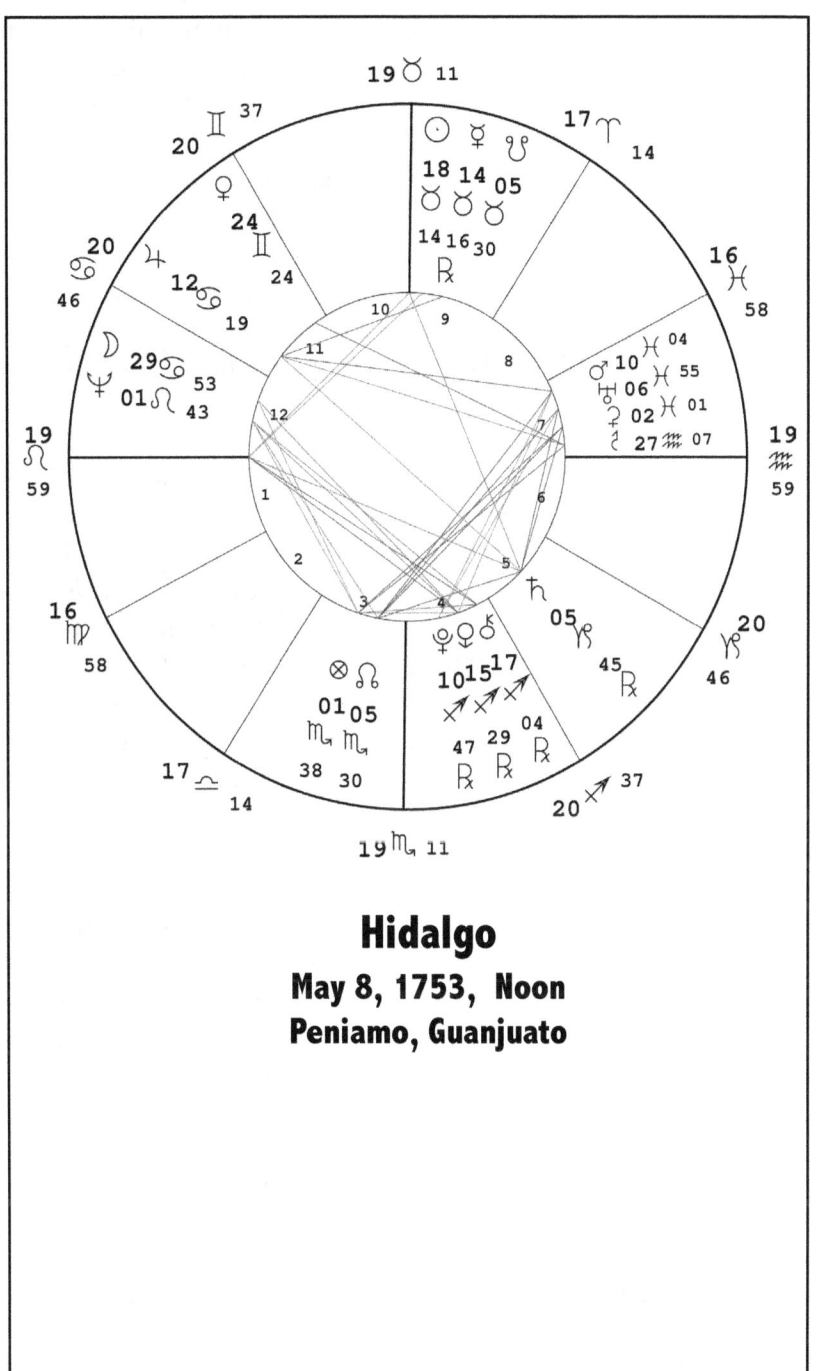

Hidalgo
May 8, 1753, Noon
Peniamo, Guanjuato

Now combine this type of modern day feeling with the old Feudal European laws of primogenitor wherein only the first son inherits the land which is the true wealth. This may sound harsh but that was the only way not to dilute the fortune, and fortune is power. If you are the third or fourth son, your only hope was to perhaps win a big battle for the king and get a land grant. At least the girls got a dowry and could hope to marry well. In Spain the laws referred to title and only the first born received it. If you were lesser nobility it was just that much worse. It is easy to see why an *hijo de algo* can relate to the less fortunate and take up the cause of the underdog. If you did buck the system during this time of history, you could get into a lot of trouble. These types of factors will tie into the life of Hidalgo himself.

If you tie the *hijo de algo* with a relationship to Saturn, a planet of karma, perhaps a person with ADD or ADHD was in trouble in the past for trying to help the oppressed, which lesser nobility may relate to. In this lifetime, with the karma of the *hijo de algo* or someone trying to help the oppressed, Saturn may suggest restriction on the ability to "function by a standard of the norm" in a learning, communicating or social setting. Each person I know (often personally and more than just persons for research for this book) with ADD or ADHD is very intelligent but is blocked or restricted (a Saturn thing) by the ADD./ADHD. It is almost a way of hiding rather than relating. It is a self-defense mechanism in their charts.

Since Hidalgo's orbit also goes almost out to Mars, there is a link between Mars and Chiron as well. Chiron's placement in a chart is often a place in need of healing. I have found that Chiron, the Nodes and Mercury also play a part with Saturn. Additionally, the Ascendant, Uranus and sometimes Neptune also play a part. Pluto often plays a strong part.

In fact almost any planet, depending on its relationship to Hidalgo or difficult aspects, can support ADD/ADHD; however, the outer planets are especially important. There is a strong eleventh and twelfth house factor. You will see this when I discuss the sample charts. **Somewhere in all of these planetary placements, Asteroid Hidalgo 944 will be a catalyst for ADD/ADHD.**

Now back to the tell—Hidalgo himself. He was born Miguel Hidalgo y Costilla or Miguel Hidalgo on May 8, 1753 in Peniamo Guanjuato. He was a *Criollo*. He was the second of four children His father was an administrator on a hacienda.

Criollo is from the Latin word *creare* meaning to create, bring into being, be born, produce, bear fruit. A *Criollo* is a type of, for lack of a better word, caste system, in the overseas colonies established by Spain. *Criollos* were Spanish, but born in the new world so were of a lesser (similar to the lesser nobility of the *hijo de algo*) than those who were born in Spain.

Since there was a shortage of Spanish women, you could also be *Criollo* if your father was born in Spain, and could have up to 1/8 indigenous blood. *Criollos* were considered far above the indigenous people, but certainly not as good as those born in Spain. Later *Criollo* nationalists were among the main supporters of the war for independence in Mexico. You can now see how being a *Criollo* was perhaps the beginning of why Hidalgo related to the less fortunate.

At age twelve Hidalgo was sent to *Colego de san Francisco Javier* to study with the Jesuits for the priesthood and was expelled. Then he went to *Colegio de San Nicolas*, the royal and pontifical university and received a degree in both philosophy and theology. He also spoke several languages, the Indian languages, French and Italian, as well as Spanish. He studied the philosophers of the Age of Enlightenment which was occurring at the time he went to college. With his ability to speak French he was able to study works such as that of Rousseau, whose philosophy taught that uncorrupted morals prevail in a state of nature. This was the antitheses of the Spanish conquering the wealth of the new world.

Hidalgo felt that man himself was good, and he did not look to the Church for approval, even though he was a priest at age 25. He did not teach the traditional Church view of the Virgin birth, celibacy or the authority of the Pope. He lived with a woman and had two daughters (so obviously the institution of marriage was a bit diluted in his mind, as well, although I have found nothing to confirm this). He was actually taken to Spain and tried at the inquisition, sent back to the new world and told to behave himself.

He then spent time on scientific work (also part of the enlightenment teachings) and tried to help the indigenous people in brick making (with an immediate return on their labors), with silk worms (a return in the near future) and in the cultivation of grape vines (a long term investment). This would give them their own wealth and thus source of power. He was able to help the indigenous people begin to create something for themselves, partially because he could keep books, taught by his father who managed a hacienda. He was trying to stop the exploitation of the lower economic echelons of society, and of course Spain would not like this because it cut into Spain's wealth and consequently, its power. This also created resentment with Spanish merchants who did things like holding reserved grain back after a drought to hike prices in an attempt to keep the indigenous people in line, rather than releasing grain as needed.

Hidalgo joined literary groups with like minds to his. In the early nineteenth century, clerics had a great deal of power, were loyal to Spain, and the indigenous people were suppressed. The literary groups eventually led to Hidaglo joining military groups, which were also joined by the Indians and Mestizos. Allende (a co-leader of the Mexican Revolution) was his co-conspirator. Hidalgo's leadership gave a spiritual quality to the revolt or a kind of religious credence so that people felt it was okay to revolt. By sheer numbers, the rebels had early victories and were moving toward Mexico City.

Hidalgo was defeated in March in Guadalajara, found guilty of treason by a military court and executed July 30, 1811 at 7:00 A.M. Herein lies the reason Hidalgo so related to those with ADD and ADHD. He was a martyr for humanity. Hidalgo was decapitated (as was Allende), and his head was on display for ten years.

Hidalgo died fighting for those in need, and I find that people who suffer ADD/ADHD were also most likely martyrs in past lives. Their martyrdom ranges from religious to military, but always on the side of a humanitarian cause. With certain placements of the asteroid Hidalgo, along with what Hidalgo as a person represented and how he died, you can see the suggestion that a person would not know how to communicate well, might have difficulty with literary skills or learning skills, then try to hide behind those difficulties as a defense mechanism in a next life—so much that medication might be needed.

This could well be a person who believed so much in a humanitarian cause that he or she laid down his/her life and suffered such a shock that now in a new time, a new life, he or she now suffers from ADD/ADHD, which is an actual physical condition, not just a phobia. As such, it goes beyond a unreasonable fear and manifests itself in the physical being of the person. Such a person is represented by Hidalgo the man, his humanitarian life and the giving of that life for others.

Hidalgo's legacy is that he was father of a nation. The chart of his execution chart is shown on page 13. That chart sums up why Asteroid 944 was named after him.

If you look at the execution chart, you will see that there are four planets in the fourth house which is the foundation, as well as the house of endings. The Part of Fortune is also here in Sagittarius. The Moon is at 29 degrees Scorpio and Mars is at 29 degrees Scorpio, indicating a lack of control over the violent situation.

Since Scorpio is the natural sign on the cusp of the eighth house, we already have psychology, investigation, karma and clandestine activity involved. Neptune is retrograde in Sagittarius and Saturn is retrograde in Sagittarius. Sagittarius naturally sits on the ninth house, so we bring in higher consciousness, religion, and humanity, karmically combined with the eighth house matters. Neptune retrograde is someone who has taken on burdens of people in a past life or is a previous fighter for the underdog, and Saturn is the planet of Karma even when not retrograde. Saturn is also obstacles. Thus, we have our martyr in his execution.

Hidalgo is a karmic life-long champion of the oppressed. Pluto retrograde in Pisces, ruled by Neptune in the fourth house, brings power struggle and reform into the reasons for his execution, and again, it is also karmic.

Jupiter is in Gemini in the tenth house so his fame and notoriety comes via his thoughts of equity and communication of his ideals. His Sun and Mercury are in the twelfth house of hidden matters and institutions but moreso they are in Leo, so this event will become very public with a showmanship quality, despite the twelfth house placement. The North Node is in the first house and among other things, Mohan Koparker compares this to a person destined to philosophical guidance.

Just a cursory look with Saturn retrograde in Sagittarius and Mars in Scorpio and Neptune Retrograde in Sagittarius in the fourth house, we can see a pattern of karmic endings based on higher consciousness and religion, etc. With Part of Fortune here, he will have a strong legacy.

If you look at the aspects, you will see further indications of the martyr. Hidalgo's execution chart has a grand cross with the Moon and Mars in the fourth house at critical 29 degrees Scorpio. Chiron is in this sixth house in Aquarius retrograde, the Midheaven is at 24 Taurus and the Ascendant is at 27 Leo. His execution is tied to a need of healing, the Midheaven suggests his notoriety and honor and his Ascendant in Leo indicates that his work and his execution will be very public. His execution will be a show.

Although not discovered in his lifetime, Eris the planet of transformation sits in the sixth house of this execution chart, along with Chiron, the healer, suggesting Hidalgo's contribution to the transformation, and his desire to heal Mexico. Both are in Aquarius, ruled by the third house Uranus in Scorpio. His actions, his teachings and his execution are very public and shake up the nation.

The execution chart also has a T-square with the Nodes square Saturn retrograde in the fourth house of endings, and Saturn in Sagittarius brings in ninth house matters of higher consciousness, religion and the like. The Part of Fortune conjunct Saturn, which I consider to indicate his legacy, and Pluto, which is retrograde in Pisces, brings into the mix a person who takes on the burdens of others and is involved in reform. With Neptune, Saturn and Pluto, all retrograde, as well as the Nodes which are karmic anyway, this execution chart takes on an air of destiny and also describes one who has fought in past lives for the right cause and is willing to die for the right cause again.

Hidalgo's life really sums up the root cause of ADD/

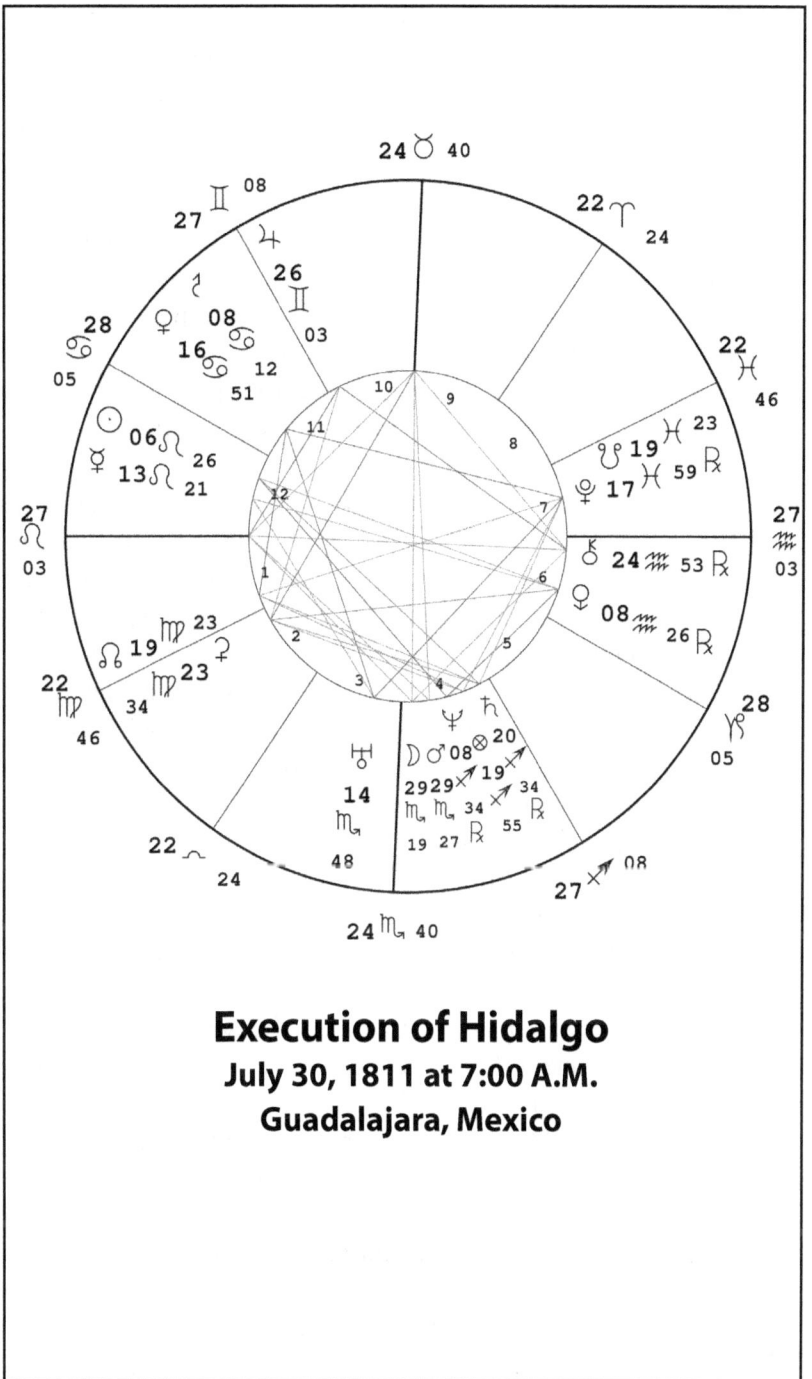

Execution of Hidalgo
July 30, 1811 at 7:00 A.M.
Guadalajara, Mexico

ADHD—someone born into a fairly comfortable life, but who is perhaps considered lesser than others due to his place of birth. He becomes a priest, but is not a very good one according to the standards of the church. He has children, lives with a woman, not adhering to the teachings of the church. He is taken to Spain for inquisition and told to be good, and is then sent home, but does not change his ways. He works for those with little or nothing to help them gain economic power–also against Spain's wishes. He becomes what would be considered by the Church as radicalized in his thoughts—though his thoughts correspond to the Age of Enlightenment. He eventually becomes militaristic in helping the unfortunate, and then finally is martyred for his cause, with his head placed on a stake after execution.

Hidalgo's story is a total sum of the ADD/ADHD person's past life conditions in one execution that lead to the defense mechanism now. This is why Asteroid 944 Hidalgo plays such an important role in the natal charts, and is the catalyst with other planets for understanding those people with ADD/ADHD.

The life of Hidalgo and what he stood for is the reason why the Mexican government requested that Asteroid 944 be named Hidalgo and why this request was granted.

The life of Hidalgo also gives us a feel for what the asteroid named Hidalgo means in astrology, and it is this meaning that can help explain the charts of ADD/ADHD persons.

Hidalgo's place in a natal chart is crucial for interpretation of ADD/ADHD. This does **not** mean that everyone who has Hidalgo in a prominent placement with other planets has ADD/ADHD, just as the fact that a placement that is the same as a celebrity means that everyone with this placement will be a celebrity. It is the preponderance of other placements combined with Hidalgo that suggest the ADD/ADHD. After looking at chart after chart, the ADD/ADHD will become apparent to you.

In this book I will look at the ADD/ADHD placements with only a partial delineation of the entire chart. My focus is on the planetary placements that are involved in ADD/ADHD. I have not found a distinction between the placements of ADD and those of ADHD. They are in fact placements of each defense mechanism.

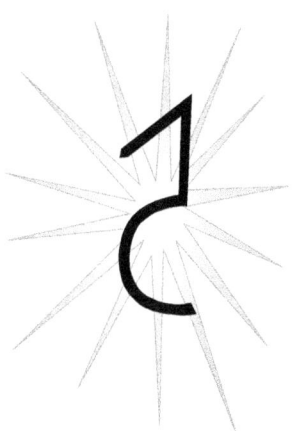

CHAPTER 2

PLANETS, NODES, HOUSES and HIDALGO

Although each planet may be positioned to relate to the ADD/ADHD placements, some have greater influence or suggest the potential for ADD/ADHD. The following definitions are how the planets and Nodes relate to ADD/ADHD placements.

Also, you may feel that the outer planets move so slowly and thus most people of a certain generation can relate to their influence on Hidalgo and this may be partly true; however, generational issues are what make history. Martyrs are often workers for the causes of their generation. With the diagnosis of ADD/ADHD, a new generation received medical treatment just as polio was eradicated with treatment of its generation. I feel that perhaps future medicines will do the same for ADD/ADHD. I think the generational diagnosis of ADD/ADHD and its karmic causes are what is important.

The **South Node** traditionally is thought to be the placement that suggests where you are coming from (past lifetimes) and the **North Node** traditionally is thought to be the placement that suggests what you are to do this lifetime. I find that the **North Node** also has past karmic ramifications, though maybe not as strong or perhaps not relating to such a distant past, but nevertheless there are karmic ramifications. I know this is not traditional but after looking at comparison charts, as well as the ADD/ADHD charts, I feel strongly about this fact. Both the North and South Nodes reflect conditions suggesting ADD and ADHD. The key to using the Nodes is balance between the two houses within which they appear. For example, if your South Node is in the tenth house of career and your North Node is in the fourth house of home and foundation, perhaps you may have been career minded and successful professionally at the expense of your home and family and now you must concentrate on this factor of your being by balancing home and career—establishing a happy medium. Your comfort zone would be tenth house matters since that is what you have done in the past, what you are used to and what you are good at. You do not want to repeat this pattern again and must learn balance. Your innate tendency is toward career and honor. If this were to combine with your ADD/ADHD placements, you may have gotten into trouble for your career or public actions at the expense of your home and family. You will see how this plays out in the definitions below.

According to Mohan Koparker, those with North Node in **the first, fifth and ninth houses** are intellectuals who aid society.

In the s**econd, sixth and tenth houses**, they aid society in economic and business matters.

In the **third, seventh and eleventh houses,** they are the peacekeepers and soldiers.

In the **fourth, eighth and twelfth houses** they are the workers who aid the other three groups.

The above definitions may help in your review of nodal placements with ADD/ADHD.

Retrograde planets are another factor in determining ADD/ADHD placements. They are also traditionally thought of as planets that, among other things, are karmic Thus, retrograde planets can offer insight into ADD/ADHD. They can suggest where you have come from and what you have to overcome now. Retrograde planets appear to move backward in the sky due to the difference in speed of planet movement. They really do not move backward but have the appearance of this from our earthly vantage point. It is an optical illusion that has to do with the relative speed of the orbits of the various planets. The appearance of backward movement suggests, in astrological interpretation, going backward or into the past. This is why I feel that retrograde planets play such an important role in ADD/ADHD.

Not all retrograde planets or nodal placements, nor all Hidalgo placements, will suggest ADD/ADHD. It is a combination of placements, or a preponderance of the placements, that lead us to the possibility of ADD/ADHD.

Also, and most importantly, in leading us to the strong suggestion of ADD/ADHD, is the placement of Asteroid 944 Hidalgo in aspect to the other planetary placements have also suggested ADD/ADHD.

Other planets that are not retrograde may be included in the placements suggesting ADD/ADHD, by virtue of their relationship to other planets or to Hidalgo.

It is the relationship or aspects of the planets, the nodes and Hidalgo that suggest ADD/ADHD. The astrological signs of the planets and houses are a consideration, but it is the planetary aspects that are of paramount importance.

DEFINITIONS—HOUSES

Since the house placements may have some significance when determining ADD/ADHD, although much less than the relationship between the planets and nodes, I will briefly define each house in order to determine how the house placement may pertain to ADD/ADHD.

First House

This house suggests how you appear to others. It is you personally. Often people will appear more as the sign on the cusp of their first house than their Sun sign. It is how you identify with yourself and the house that suggests your automatic reactions. One such automatic reaction could be ADD/ADHD.

Cusp
This is the dividing line between the houses. The sign on the Cusp of your first house or the dividing line between the twelfth house and the first house is your Ascendant. The Ascendant embodies first house impressions.

Second House
This is the house of money and possessions, how you earn your income and tangible assets. More importantly for ADD/ADHD, it is the house of your own personal values.

Third House
This is the house of conscious mind, lower education, communication, brothers and sisters. Since this is the house of conscious mind, it may hold clues to ADD/ADHD as well.

Fourth House
This is the home and foundation, as well as your ancestors. It suggests your emotional needs. Anything in the past that affected this house could well hold suggestions for ADD/ADHD.

Fifth House
This is the house of creativity, romance, speculation, children, games, hobbies. Any of these activities could have karmic ramifications. For example, did your radical art get you into tremendous trouble in the past and could you avoid expression now because of this?

Sixth House
This is the house of work, service, health, pets, employees and any type of detail. Obviously, the house of health may hold clues to ADD/ADHD. This is a strong indicator house of ADD/ADHD.

Seventh House
This is the house of contracts, any legal binding document, marriage and grandparents. Perhaps contractual relationships got you into trouble in the past or perhaps you were too headstrong and

outspoken in the past with your spouse and you are now fearful of expressing yourself, suggesting ADD/ADHD as a defense.

Eighth House
This is the house of government, insurance, intimacy, shared assets, death, taxes, hidden matters. You can well imagine that any one of these things could be suggestive of ADD/ADHD. For example, how and why did you die in the past?

Ninth House
This is the house of higher education, personal philosophy, religion, the judicial branch of the government, science and anything foreign - be it travel or matters or objects. This is one of the houses I have found really influences ADD/ADHD and the matters in life that this house stands for suggest the same. Historically, how many people have gotten into trouble for their religion? How many college professors throughout history have gotten into trouble for speaking out?

Tenth House
This is the house of profession, career, honors, authority, and may suggest the executive branch of the government. Okay - it is becoming obvious - executive branch of government, did you get into trouble for actions deemed anti-government? Did your career or profession get you into trouble - perhaps speaking out and using its power? These could be indicators of ADD/ADHD.

Eleventh House
This is the house of friends, groups, wishes for the future, organizations and the legislature. Again, belonging to a group considered hostile to a government or perhaps outlawed by the government (legislature) may have caused you trouble in the past. This is also the house of finances and values to your house of career (using derivative houses which I do with a few houses in ADD/ADHD placements) and thus, your use of company assets or expressing company values may also have been trouble.

Twelfth House

This is the house of the subconscious, hidden conditions, institutions such as prison and hospitals, and escapism. There is probably not one manifestation of this house that would not suggest ADD/ADHD.

I have found that houses 9 through 12, then 3 and 6 are large influences on ADD/ADHD. **The use of aspects and especially the use of midpoints placed in these houses conjunct a planet are of utmost importance.**

THE PLANETS

Sun

The Sun is where your strength lies and the house within which it is placed is very important. It suggests where your self esteem will be. Its placement is where you will shine. If the Sun is part of ADD/ADHD placement, you should have the strength to overcome, cope with, and flourish despite the ADD/ADHD.

Moon

The Moon suggests changes and your emotions. It suggests motherly or care-taking traits. Thus, if contained in ADD/ADHD placements, there is a suggestion of past care-taking difficulty or past emotional changes that contribute to the ADD/ADHD.

Mercury

Mercury deals with thought processes, conscious mind and communication. It stands to reason that this planet may be linked to ADD/ADHD placements but not as heavily as you may think. Although Mercury may be linked, other planet links seem stronger. When Mercury combines with other planets in an ADD/ADHD placement, then the reasoning for the ADD/ADHD is apparent. Saturn, Neptune and Uranus are as important, and often Pluto as well.

Mercury Retrograde suggests trouble for speaking out in a past life. Thus, you now use ADD or ADHD as a defense mechanism. You have trouble communicating and/or learning on a cognitive level. This is not an intelligence matter, it is a matter of not communicating or learning by subconscious choice. How can you be in trouble for something physical? This keeps fear of communication at a distance. Often Mercury retrograde suggests excellent concentration, but with other ADD/ADHD placements you are distracted by everything around you. Thus, the Mercury retrograde is often in combination with other placements that demonstrate why you have the ADD/ADHD now. Even with the ADD/ADHD, you may be in tune with the universal consciousness ,which is a double-edged sword. You may want to speak out again and even do so, while the ADD/ADHD continues to plague you. You feel apart from society with the ADD\ADHD.

Venus

Venus suggests your desire for pleasure, beauty, luxury and comfort. It suggests charm and perhaps looking for an easy way to work. Venus is a benevolent planet and if it is a planet connected to planets in your ADD/ADHD placements, it will help make the journey more smooth for you.

Venus Retrograde suggests past difficulty with relationships. Perhaps your mate seemed to always come up short in your eyes. Perhaps for some reason you were not able to be with your partner and the relationship suffered. These are not necessarily things that I have found lead to the ADD/ADHD markers. Although if Venus retrograde is connected with other markers now, it may affect your current relationships so that the past is repeated somehow.

Mars

Mars suggests independence, drive and spirit, but also combativeness or the warrior. Thus, Mars linked to ADD\ADHD placements will give you drive to overcome obstacles but you may also feel angry about this situation. Your spirit will help you prevail if you focus on the positive side of Mars.

Mars Retrograde: You are trying to overcome past conditions of perhaps a warrior who was on what may have been considered by those in power, the wrong side of the human issue, a ruthless warrior who had to fight for everything and perhaps lost quite a bit in the process. Your feelings are linked to the past, and you are trying through shear strength to overcome these feelings. Rather than misdirecting action, you have chosen, in a sense, to misdirect your brain activity—as a defense. You are paying for something in your past in a very personal way.

Jupiter

Jupiter deals with higher understanding, spirituality, opportunity, expansion, but also over-zealousness, too high expectations and ideals of yourself or others. It is your optimism.

Jupiter Retrograde suggests that perhaps you spoke out for ideals or religious beliefs in the past and now you may be afraid to do so again. Perhaps you got into a great deal of trouble for this. As such, this may be a placement that involves dealing with ADD/ADHD. However, if Jupiter is involved, you should have the opportunity to overcome or deal with the ADD/ADHD. Also, since Jupiter means expansion, the ADD/ADHD may be expansive. Opportunity and expansion are two sides of the ADD/ADHD issue when Jupiter retrograde is involved.

SATURN AND THE OUTER PLANETS

The outer planets play a large part in ADD/ADHD placements and I feel they suggest generational happenings, of which you were a large part, that led to the defense mechanism of ADD/ADHD in this lifetime. My discussion of Asteroid 944 Hidalgo will reinforce this theory. Thus, I will spend a little more time discussing Saturn, Neptune, Uranus and Pluto and a great deal of time discussing Asteroid 944 Hidalgo.

Saturn

Saturn is a planet of karma, even when direct. Saturn is boundaries and restrictions, whether self-imposed, imposed by others or by circumstances, and it keeps your unlimited desires in check. Saturn is associated with dread. Saturn will not allow you to deny your own shortcomings. It is a source of your self-criticism, and is also is where you begin to work hard for long term success. It is a place to learn patience. Thus, whenever you have a Saturn return, you can either grow and reap the rewards from what you have built, and continue into the next phase of your life, or you can fail and come to terms with your lack of work and start again.

Saturn is life lessons, and represents barriers you wish to overcome. Saturn is also quite positive, in that it is where you do learn discipline. It should not necessarily be viewed in the negative but as a place and a chance to improve.

Saturn Retrograde: Take the above Saturn definitions which are quite karmic and multiply them tenfold. Saturn retrograde is intense, and you will feel great obstacles and restrictions. There is no doubt that you will repeat your past Saturn influenced actions, but in a different setting or context, and hopefully will grow this time. Saturn is the teacher and this is your chance to learn. Saturn is actually a door to the outer planets and links the inner planets to the outer ones.

Saturn retrograde is your link to overcoming or learning to deal with ADD/ADHD. If you have this planet retrograde in your natal chart, you may have been abused by those in power, or you yourself may have been the one with the misused power. Thus, if you spoke out about any wrongdoing, be it political, religious and the like, you may have been incarcerated and mistreated. You may or may not have been on the side of humanity, but in the case of the ADD/ADHD placements, I have found that the individuals were on the side of the poor, the mistreated, or the underdog, so to speak. They were part of a generation working toward positive change.

Whether Saturn is direct or retrograde, its karmic ramifications appear to play an important role in charts of people with ADD/ADHD, either specifically by placement or by link with Hidalgo and other planets.

Lynn Koiner concludes that the Prefrontal Cortex of the brain (Saturn) is associated with ADD and ADHD. Thus, Saturn is very influential in both a medical and karmic sense.

Uranus

Uranus is in each astrological sign for about seven years Thus, it suggests generational issues, although house placement can bring Uranus into personal traits, as well. Uranus is the rebel. A strong Uranus suggests a reformer. Uranus is chaos. I often describe Uranus like throwing a deck of cards into the air, and they fall where they may. In other words, here is a lack of ability to control. Also (in my mind), Uranus has strong suggestions of the metaphysical. This planet's house placement can help determine where the Uranus traits apply, but it is difficult to second guess a Uranus placement.

Uranus Retrograde suggests inner chaos and also difficulty with relationships. In a past life you were definitely the rebel—be it for good or bad causes. In the case of ADD/ADHD persons, you were the rebel for a good cause but chaos ruled the times. The powers that be did not agree with you. You would fight the establishment. Now you must learn to give a little in order to gain a lot. Also, your past life was dominated with your causes and now you must learn to have a life outside your fight of the good fight.

In ADD/ADHD placements, Uranus now suggests a chaos of the mind. This is your defense against past persecution. You are to form new mental abilities and thought processes which may again create a rebel leader, but you are trying hard to distance yourself with the ADD/ADHD.

Neptune

Neptune suggests mediumistic opportunity. It is the common psyche of your generation, what you are innately attuned to, and it suggests indefinable feelings of your generation. It also has a negative side which suggests you may take on the problems, insecurities and feelings of those around you. Thus, you may take on the ills of your generation and try to conquer them. Also, there may be an indication of substance abuse or overindulgence. Creativity is a wonderful expression of Neptune.

If Neptune is part of your ADD/ADHD placement, perhaps you got into trouble for taking on the angst of your generation and bucking the establishment. You probably knew you would be in trouble but did it anyway, It takes Neptune thirteen to fourteen years to go through an astrological sign.

Neptune retrograde: Escapism probably was a problem in past lives, to the extent perhaps of drugs, alcohol and experimentation. Also, you may have used your core creativity to speak out, i.e. radical artwork in a repressive society, and gotten into very big trouble for it. Your penchant to help others and to help in things important to your generation may have been at the expense of helping your own spiritual potential. Thus, you now seek the defense mechanism that keeps you from cognitively coping, but deep down you are still finding the right way for the world. You rely on your intuition now rather than actually trying to communicate "like everyone else."

Pluto

Pluto may be in an astrological sign as little as twelve years and as much as thirty-two years. Pluto suggests the shared ideas of a generation, shared mores, shared politics, pretty much all shared markers of a generation. Since this planet is so generational, you can see how it may relate to promulgating the ideals of your generation in a public way, and this may have caused you trouble in the past. Pluto is also control and power issues. Again, things that can get you into trouble. Pluto is often part of ADD/ADHD placements. Pluto's theme suggests transformation and upheaval. It is tantamount to do or die.

Pluto Retrograde: You may have been in trouble for group activities or were shunned by the group. There can be a scapegoat quality to the retrograde Pluto. If you were indeed a scapegoat in any type of violent way, ADD/ADHD can become your defense this time around. You may not trust others, so will use your ADD/ADHD to avoid communication or to lead people to feel you are not capable. This, then, becomes your power now.

Ceres

Ceres has an orbit between Mars and Jupiter and is thought to contain water and ice. Thus, the idea that Ceres is the nurturer (with water and ice) seems very plausible. Ceres suggests nurturing whether you nurture others, how you accept nurturing or your perception of what nurturing should be. In light of ADD/

ADHD, it may suggest how nurture helps you deal with it. Ceres also represents an absence of nurturing.

Ceres retrograde suggests past conditions and perhaps your getting into trouble nurturing the oppressed and helping them to advance, which was not accepted by the powers that be. It appears that Ceres may be somewhat more involved with ADD/ADHD than Eris. Ceres placement may help one cope with ADD/ADHD

Eris

According to Tom Canfield, author of *Yankee Doodle Discord,* a book about this new planet, Eris is difficult and when conjunct may act as a friend but turn out to be an enemy. He uses historical events to support his work. He is working with Eris at mundane level. His times in history are times of transformation. Lynn Koiner's research attributed transformation to Eris. I feel that transformation is often difficult, so historically it appears hard no matter what the aspect. Lynn did not find conjunction as a difficult aspect personally.

Lynn Koiner has found Eris to be transformational and benefic on a persona level. If you are rigid and unable to compromise or adapt, you may have trouble. Since transformation is often personally difficult, in light of ADD/ADHD, I think transformation is the key here. Did you, in a past life, help the oppressed transform their position? Per Koiner, "hard aspects from Uranus-Pluto, Eris does not seem like a benefit, but its challenges allow us to transform our lives—and therein, it is a benefic."

Eris tends to compliment Pluto in actions of tear down, reform and rebuild.

Of course, Eris and Ceres join the outer planets in generational themes, in addition to the personal level interpretations in individual charts.

Asteroid 944 Hidalgo

Aside from the life of Hidalgo discussed previously, it is important to know that the asteroid takes fourteen years to travel around the zodiac. Its path is very eccentric and **it spends about 50% of its time in two signs.** This is very important. The signs are Scorpio.

in which it spends about 3.36 years, and Sagittarius in which it spends 3.6 years. On the other hand it only spends 42 days in Gemini, or about 8% of its time. If you think about this, it makes a lot of sense, in light of the ADD/ADHD connection.

Scorpio rules the eighth house of, among other things, psychology and hidden matters. Sagittarius rules the ninth house of higher consciousness, religion and philosophy. Thus, working for something of higher consciousness or for humanity, and perhaps in a hidden or secretive manner, may have gotten you into trouble in past lives.

Combine this with only 42 days in Gemini which rules the third house of conscious mind, learning and communication. You can then see why such little time in Gemini may indicate that the conscious mind is deeply affected by the psychological ramifications of past action based on your higher consciousness, with little time to cope with your conscious mind matters.

Also, Hidalgo is an asteroid of Karma *vis a vis* ADD/ADHD. Always keep this in mind when delineating a natal chart.

THE ASTROLOGICAL SIGNS

I feel that the planetary relationships are a much stronger indication of ADD/ADHD markers than the sign or the houses within which they are placed. The astrological signs still contribute, especially if strong in a chart, so I will briefly define the signs as well. Also, look to the rulers of signs as keys to ADD/ADHD placements also. Keywords for the twelve astrological signs are as follows:

Aries
Aries is a cardinal fire sign ruled by Mars. Traits are a self-starter, lots of energy, enthusiasm, quick action. On the other side of the coin, there is the Mars combativeness and working too hard, as well as a bit of self-centeredness.

Taurus
Taurus is a fixed, earth sign, ruled by Venus, that suggests a practical, creative, dependable person who also loves luxury and

can be very over-indulgent. Taurus placements indicate one who is loyal, and tends to always feel that he or she is right.

Gemini
Gemini is a mutable, air sign ruled by Mercury. This sign suggests adaptability, the ability to multi-task and a quick mind, but one who might also be high strung with nervous energy.

Cancer
Cancer is a cardinal, water sign that is ruled by the Moon. Cancer suggests sympathy, emotions, a romantic, retentiveness and insecurity, but most of all, a nurturer. Cancer also has a great memory for detail.

Leo
Leo is a fixed, fire sign ruled by the Sun. Leo is the actor and sportsman of the zodiac. Leo is the risk taker and will do what it takes to put himself or herself in the limelight. Leo has a great deal of energy, and is both confident and likable.

Virgo
Virgo is a mutable, earth sign ruled by Mercury. Virgo suggests a person that is analytical, meticulous, cautious, shy and health-oriented. Virgo placements may indicate a step-by-step worker, who may work in the background while someone else receives the accolades.

Libra
Libra is a cardinal, air sign ruled by Venus. Libra suggests that you may be indecisive, non-aggressive, artistic, adaptable, temperamental, just and charming. You may feel that you must do and/or manage more than one thing at a time. You may work with a partner and are able to see both sides of an issue.

Scorpio
Scorpio is a fixed, water sign ruled by Mars and Pluto. Scorpio suggests one who is suspicious, magnetic, penetrating, sarcastic, jealous, domineering, intuitive, persevering, loyal and powerful.

You go below the surface and see the whole picture, even the very dark side of the picture.

Sagittarius

Sagittarius is a mutable, fire sign ruled by Jupiter. Sagittarius suggests self-righteousness, dogmatic, restless, scattered, hopeful, giving, optimistic and idealistic. Travel and foreign matters are important. Higher education is involved. This can be the religious monk and the philosopher.

Capricorn

Capricorn, a cardinal, earth sign, is ruled by Saturn. Capricorn indicates self-discipline, seriousness, rigidity, caution, secretiveness, responsibility and cynicism. Capricorn is about as down to earth as you can get.

Aquarius

Aquarius is a fixed, air sign ruled by Uranus. Aquarius suggests that you are self-sufficient and a visionary, in respect to ideals rather than by "seeing a vision," or in being a reformer, or one who is rebellious and impersonal. Aquarius reminds me of the machine-like nerd who is amazing and may seem almost like part of his or her computer.

Pisces

Pisces is a mutable, water sign ruled by Neptune. Pisces is trusting, adaptable, dreamy, empathetic, moody, artistic and psychic. Pisceans tend to take on the problems of those around them. They also must watch for substance abuse.

CHAPTER 3

ADD/ADHD PLACEMENTS IN INDIVIDUAL CHARTS

There will appear to be a lot of repetition in this chapter and in chapter 4, as well. Remember, it is the preponderance of astrological placements that may indicate ADD/ADHD. Just one placement does not do it alone. Thus, there is a great repetition of themes.

It will appear as though there is a circling pattern which involves eighth and ninth house influences. This may be seen either by sign, house or ruler, or outer planets and some inner planets, but all of which relate to Hidalgo as a catalyst.

EVAN

Evan (whose chart is on page 31) was born April 21, 1965 at 11:58 P.M., in Los Angeles, California. He has a Ph.D. in Psychology.

Evan's Hidalgo is at 29 degrees Libra—a critical degree. Twenty-nine degrees is a crises oriented point. It is a place where decision making is difficult, creating a plan of action is difficult and there is lots of planning but excessive worry. It may be the

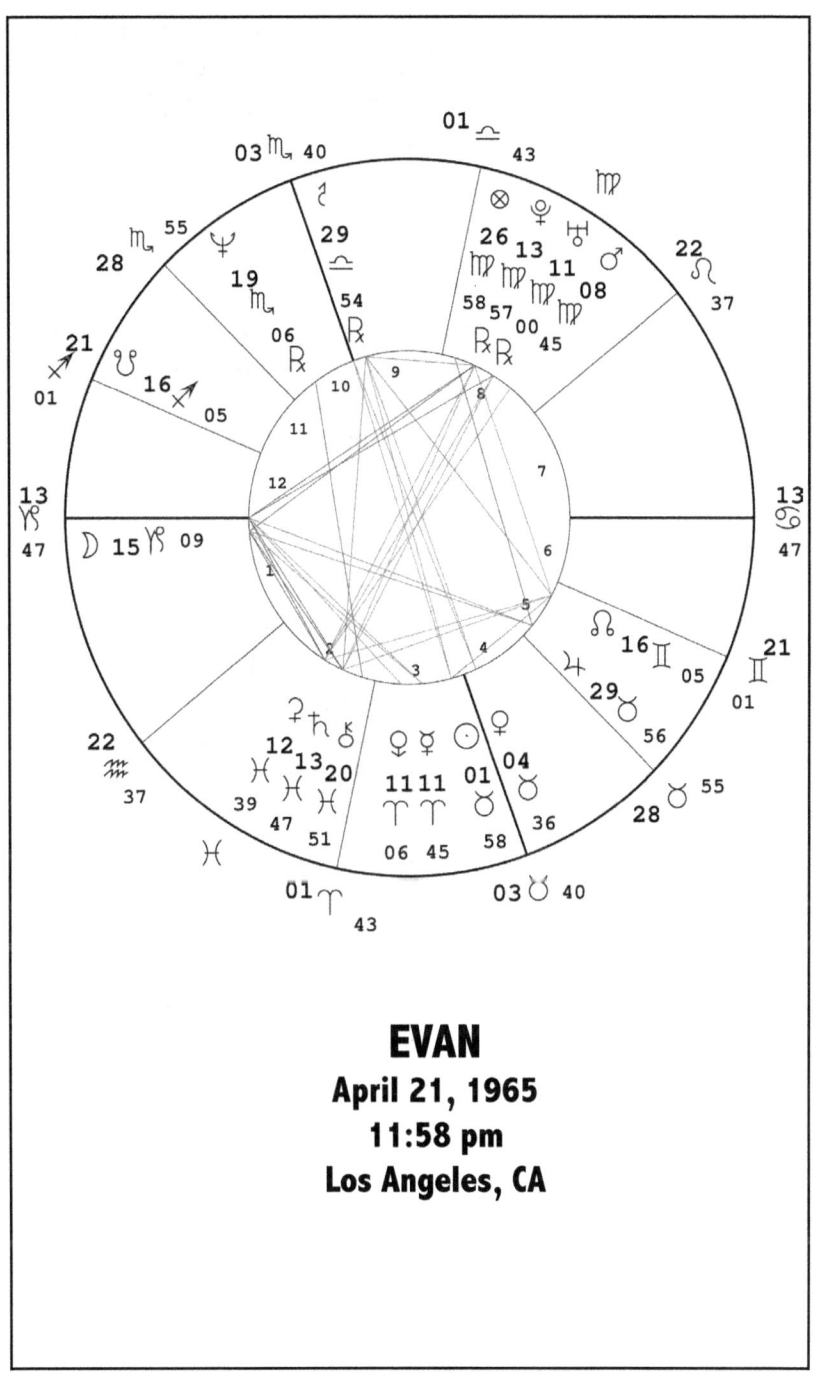

EVAN
April 21, 1965
11:58 pm
Los Angeles, CA

weakest point of a sign. For Evan, this is also combined with the sign of Libra which is indecisive and seeks justice. Hidalgo is in the ninth house of higher conscious philosophy, which you will see adds to the Hidalgo effect of this ADD chart. Libra suggests a going back and forth over issues which may contribute to the inattentiveness of ADHD.

Since Hidalgo is in the ninth house, we can see where Evan may have been in trouble in the past for speaking out about religious issues, or about higher philosophical issues relating to the underdog. Or perhaps he was persecuted in a foreign country, or was persecuted just for his ideals in his own country. Most importantly, since Hidalgo is in Libra, he was probably in legal trouble for his actions.

Both Pluto and Uranus in this chart are retrograde in the eighth house, so we can see where generational chaos, reform and the like probably were his downfall. He may have worked behind the scenes for reform, since Pluto is the ruler of Scorpio and Scorpio is the natural cusp of the eighth house, as well.

The Part of Fortune and Sun are conjunct in the third house at 0 and 1 degrees Taurus, which is opposite the Hidalgo in the ninth house and is the first strong indication of Evan's profession, which ties into the Hidalgo idea of helping. He is an addiction counselor. His higher consciousness is speaking for or helping with those who are addicted. The strength of his Sun and his Part of Fortune in his communication house are enhanced by Hidalgo, so that he speaks out for those who are oppressed. Or, in his case, with his third house Taurus Sun, this may also include those who are overindulgent and viewed badly by society as a result.

Because Part of Fortune and Sun are in the third house, Evan is able to communicate well and to speak for others with problems, despite his ADD/ADHD. In fact, his ADD/ADHD is probably one reason that he went into counseling as a profession. Often people with ADD try to self medicate before diagnosis and being properly seen by a doctor, especially those who had difficulties before ADD/ADHD became a commonly known condition. Hidalgo in opposition to Evan's third house placements suggest impairment of some kind, or the ADD/ADHD from which he suffers.

Hidalgo is at the midpoint of Uranus at 11 Virgo in the eighth house and South Node at 16 Sagittarius in the eleventh house. This again ties to psychology, with chaotic Uranus in the eighth house and the karmic South Node in Sagittarius. This may relate to his having been speaking out for the underdog or for religious beliefs, in a former incarnation—especially since Sagittarius is the natural ruler of the ninth house wherein lies Hidalgo this time around. Hidalgo brings the past life condition of Uranus and the South Node together. The Sagittarius actions combine with Uranus in Virgo, a down to earth sign, suggesting hard conditions creating ADD/ADHD placements this lifetime. Any placement in Sagittarius tied with Hidalgo is a suggestion of ADD/ADHD since Sagittarius is the natural ruler of the ninth house of values, higher consciousness and the like.

Pluto is conjunct Uranus in the eighth house and thus is another factor in the placement of Hidalgo at the Pluto and South Node midpoint. Both Pluto and Uranus are retrograde, reinforcing this placement of someone who was in trouble for speaking out or working for the oppressed on humanitarian, generational issues, and now has become a counselor for those who are looked down upon this time around. Still, he also suffers from ADD/ADHD because of his past actions. Mars in Virgo suggests military action, and since it is conjunct Uranus retrograde and Pluto retrograde in the eighth house, I feel that Evan's past martyrdom may have been as a military person on the humanitarian side of a war.

There is a Grand Square with Saturn at 13 Pisces in the second house (money and personal values), the North Node in the fifth house in Gemini (representing the mind), the South Node at 16 Sagittarius (past life conditions of higher values). Then Uranus at 10 Virgo and Pluto at 13 Virgo, both retrograde in the eighth house, represent the power struggle and complete the Grand Square. Saturn and Pluto are opposite to the exact degree. Here we have Saturn, of great karma, in the personal house of values square Pluto and Uranus in the house of, amongst other things, psychology or psychiatry. The South Node is suggesting past conditions of championing higher consciousness ideals, while North Node in Gemini represents the conscious mind.

What could be more karmic and more apparent as to Evan's ADD/ADHD placements! This alone, with planetary relationships to Hidalgo, pretty much screams ADD/ADHD. Also, it is important to note that Ceres is conjunct Saturn and thus is associated with such heavy ADD/ADHD placements as well. This may help Evan to cope. It may also affect Evan's desire to help or nurture others for his profession.

While I feel that Evan's Hidalgo at 29 critical degrees in Libra at the midpoint of Uranus/Pluto, and with the karmic South Node in Sagittarius as natural sign of the ninth house, is the most telling placement of his ADD/ADHD, I feel the other placements discussed show how he works out his ADD/ADHD placements in the present. He could be a teacher of difficult or learning disabled children, as well as an addiction counselor. He would feel good about himself with either profession. His profession in psychology goes a long way to help him overcome difficult feelings created by an ADD/ADHD childhood.

Also important in Evan's chart are the following placements: Mercury is at 11 Aries in his third house. Mercury is also at the midpoint between the Sun at 1 Taurus in the third house and Chiron in the second house at 20 Pisces. This suggests strength in communication with Aries energy and forcefulness, but Chiron shows a place that needs healing. In Pisces in the second house, Chiron suggests that perhaps the need for healing is due to his personal values. Pisces intuitiveness can now help the communication of Mercury in the third house by Evan's ability to heal through communication. More importantly is the second house relationship to values, so Evan's values are crucial to his communication skills and also to his ability to heal himself and others through those skills. These placements help him cope with ADD/ADHD.

Evan's Eris is conjunct Mercury in the third house of communication, and through words, now he is trying to transform the lives of others.

However, Chiron is conjunct Saturn in Pisces by a wide orb. Since both Chiron and Saturn are in the second house of values, and Saturn suggests karmic ramifications, Evan needs healing based on deep personal values. With Pisces, he again will take on the problems of others—kind of like repeating the past. He has an intuitive set of values based on the past. Therefore, he must be aware of this and avoid repeating old patterns.

The North Node at 16 Gemini in the fifth house is midpoint between Uranus at 10 Virgo in the eighth house and Chiron at 20 Pisces in the second house. Gemini is the mind, and with Uranus and Chiron (or chaos and a need of healing), again we can see the placements of ADD/ADHD. The personal values of second house and eighth house matters come into play with the ADD/ADHD.

Psychology can be read from the eighth house and creativity from the fifth house. Both are good ways to cope with the ADD/ADHD. More importantly to Evan, the fifth house is, among other things, the house of gambling. I feel that his counseling of addiction, including gambling addiction, is a good way to find relief from the ADD\ADHD.

Evan's eighth house contains a three point stellium of Mars, Uranus and Pluto, all in Virgo. This is a lot of energy, chaos and reorganization in eighth house matters, and is very good for a psychologist. Although these placements create havoc with the ADD/ADHD placements I've pointed out, they also reinforce patterns of past lives in a positive way through counseling.

The Ascendant at 13 Capricorn is at the midpoint of Chiron in the second house and the Midheaven at 3 Scorpio, so we now have a personal placement in between houses relating to healing and profession, with Scorpio and Pisces involved, although it stretches just a little bit my usual rule of no more than a 1 degree orb for midpoints. This one brings a lot of intuition into the mix.

Moon (of emotion and in Capricorn, relating to earthly matters), is in the first house in Capricorn conjunct Ascendant, and is within acceptable orb of the midpoints Saturn/Neptune and Neptune/Chiron. (I normally use a one degree orb for midpoints, but I am extending it here to three degrees to include Moon since this configuration is so particularly descriptive.)

All of these midpoints reinforce the ADD\ADHD placements, especially with the Chiron placement included. They also reinforce Evan's career, which helps him cope with his ADD\ADHD.

Evan has a square key which is very telling in his chart. The square and inconjunct is lessened by the trine which helps him a bit. Moon is square Mercury, and Moon is trine Uranus and Pluto. Mercury is inconjunct Uranus and Pluto. Also, the South Node (his karmic past) is square Pluto and Uranus. The trine helps lessen the tension of the tremendous squares, but not enough to keep Evan from having a very difficult time with his ADD/ADHD.

Remember, Uranus and Pluto are retrograde, so there are heavy past life conditions here, and the other aspects, aside from the relationship to Hidalgo, suggest or reinforce the ADD/ADHD.

Again, Uranus and Pluto are retrograde in Virgo in the eighth house—a very karmic placement— and they are also square the South Node in the eleventh house in Sagittarius. Uranus and Pluto are part of the square key. The Eighth house Uranus retrograde suggests difficult personal relationships, while at the same time helping others understand themselves. Evan may be very introverted, even through relating to others. He is looking for mental clarity which he may not find with ADD\ADHD, so he must guard against quickly changing direction—perhaps several times in a few minutes. Patience is lacking and he wants everything too quickly. He must put his quick ideas into order and then into practicality within his life. Spirituality will help.

With Pluto in the eighth house, Evan is trying to also reorganize the values of those he is in contact with. He is clinical. Is there any wonder why he is a therapist? He is actually able, with the use of his own personal power, to concentrate internally, but he is erratic with the external.

Neptune is retrograde at 10 Scorpio, and here it suggests confusion in attainment of goals; but also a deep creativity and a deep psychic ability. Evan will not be happy until he finds peace in himself. External success, alone, won't give him this. More importantly, Neptune retrograde in Scorpio can be a wonderful therapist who helps others grow into who they should be, discarding past baggage—this is a true visionary.

Evan's T-Square containing Neptune is combined within his ADD/ADHD placements, especially in how they relate to Hidalgo.

They are Saturn, North Node, South Node, Uranus and Pluto and this T-square just reinforces the ADD\ADHD placements.

Evan's placements strongly indicate his ADD\ADHD but those same planets and placements also indicate his profession, which will be a great help with the ADD\ADHD. He has a t-edged sword.

DARIUS

Darius (whose chart is on page 39) was born July 16, 1978, at 12:35 pm in Los Angeles. He is an attorney.

Chiron at 9 Taurus in the Seventh House is the midpoint between Midheaven at 18 Cancer and Part of Fortune in the fifth house at 29 Aquarius—a critical point suggesting no control. Chiron is also at the midpoint of Jupiter at 19 Cancer 15 in the Tenth House and Part of Fortune. More importantly, Chiron (with that midpoint) is also opposite Uranus, which is retrograde in Scorpio in the first house. So, there is personal, as well as karmic chaos affected by a place in need of healing.

Since Scorpio is the natural ruler of the eighth house, we are seeing (with the above mentioned placements), eighth house potentials such as secretive activities, government, psychology, research and death factoring in with the unsuspected and chaos brought about by past karma. Uranus is conjunct his second house of personal values and since Uranus is retrograde, the values are based on past generational themes.

Jupiter in the tenth house brings in factors of career, fortune and expansion, again with a place in need of healing which is trine Uranus, retrograde in Scorpio, so this is personal. Since Uranus is conjunct the second house cusp, this tells me that at some point in time, with Uranus retrograde, Darius was very personally in trouble for the chaos he caused (probably based on his personal value system) that did not coincide with the powers that be. Also, with Uranus in Scorpio, he probably worked behind the scenes for reform. There were power struggles, and this is emphasized by a need for healing now. Since Chiron is in Taurus, he will feel the need to heal on a very earthly level.

Darius has his Midheaven in Cancer, so his foundation (shown by Capricorn on his IC, the fourth house cusp) played a part in his fame, honor or dishonor, as it also will today and going forward. In fact, Uranus opposite Chiron is a large contributor to his ADD/ADHD. Uranus, of course, can be the chaotic energy and the hyperactivity that affects him personally.

With the Sun in his tenth house, Darius will shine in his career and this will help offset insecurity because of the ADD/ADHD.

Mercury is inconjunct the cusp on Darius' sixth house of health, so mental health or his mind not working as other peoples' minds do is somewhat suggested, but not as much as would be expected with ADD/ADHD.

Saturn is at the midpoint between Pluto at 14 Libra in the twelfth house and the Midheaven at 18 Cancer, (I may use a 3 degree orb w/Saturn and possibly Neptune, Uranus or Pluto since they move so slowly). This may indicate a link between career based on foundational matters (Midheaven is in Cancer), with the power and reorganization of Pluto in the twelfth house of subconscious, and the heavy karma of Saturn.

Saturn is in Leo in the eleventh house of among other things, groups, and in Leo, this is the actor or the person in the limelight.

Doesn't this sound like perhaps Darius at some point in time used his career or power to help a group champion something that he felt was very important on a foundational level?

Also, with Pluto in Libra in the twelfth house he may have tried to reorganize the group or reorganize society and gotten into trouble for it. Since Pluto is in the house of hidden enemies, and Libra suggests legal matters, he may have been imprisoned. If so, this is based on the karma of Saturn. He also has to watch similar activities today, with his current chart, so he does not get into trouble. His job today also champions the individual via the group.

Added to the above, Mars is at an 18 Virgo midpoint between Mercury at 20 Leo in the tenth house and Ascendant at 16 Libra. Mars is in the eleventh house of groups and in Virgo, suggests military and his speech in this current life, and this may also be

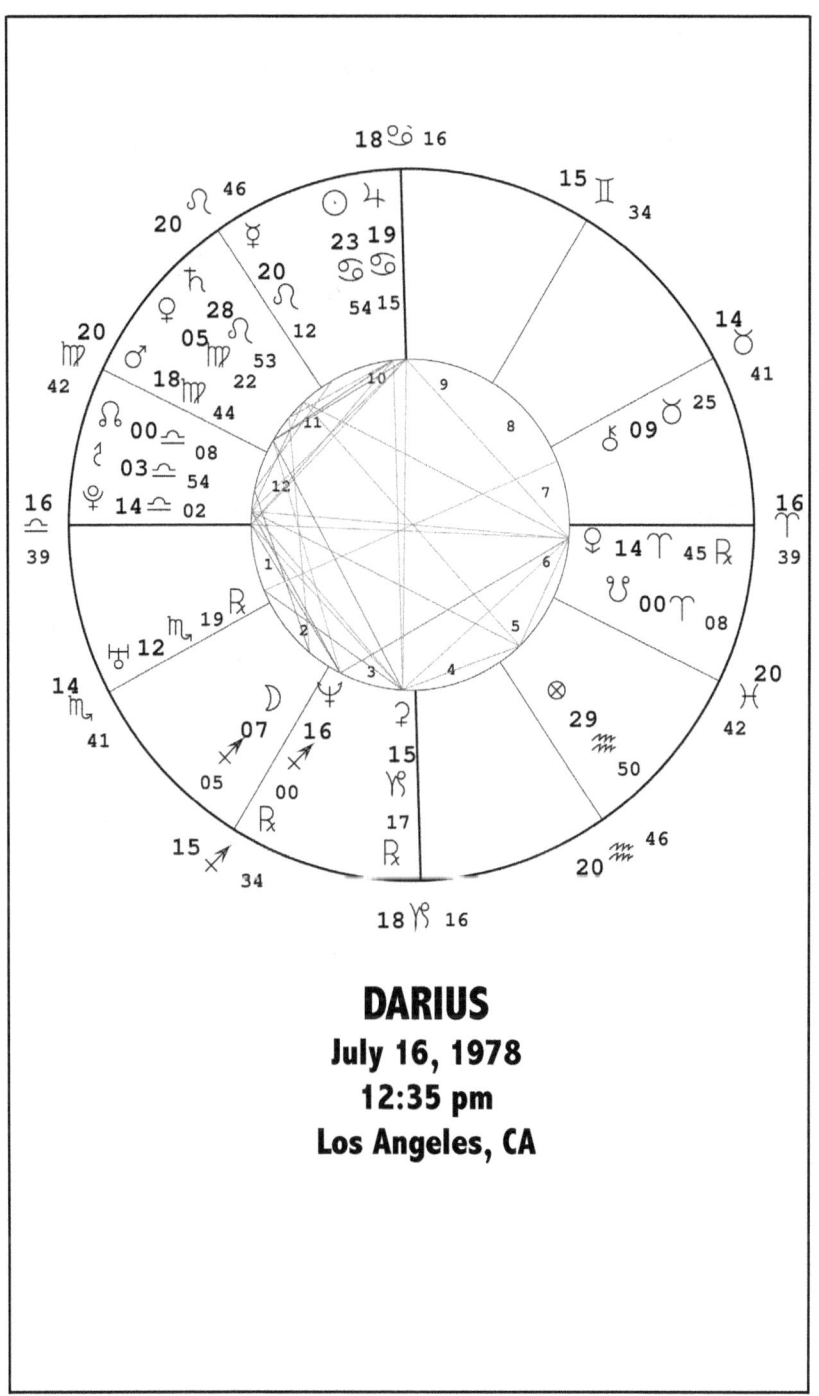

DARIUS
July 16, 1978
12:35 pm
Los Angeles, CA

affected by his subconscious. Again, with Pluto in Libra, the subconscious mind could suggest legal matters or imprisonment or some type of institution in a past life.

His Mercury is in Leo in the tenth house, which now suggests someone who speaks out and is comfortable doing so. Darius can be a showman. These planets are not retrograde, so he must watch what he does in this lifetime, so he will avoid repeating actions from the past that would cause his ADD/ADHD to flare up again.

His retrograde planets are Uranus and Neptune, however, any planet in the twelfth house of subconscious will carry past life conditions if they relate to ADD/ADHD in the present. Pluto in the twelfth in Libra suggests a past reformer or a power struggle of someone seeking balance and equality.

North Node in the twelfth house is very telling at the 0 degree in Libra—a cardinal point on the midpoint of Moon at 7 degrees Sagittarius in the second house and the Sun at 23 degrees Cancer in the tenth house. Moon is in Sagittarius in the second house of values, so Darius' values are based on higher consciousness, religion, higher values and the like. His Sun is in the tenth house, so he must do something that does not conflict with his values. This, with the North Node, is suggestive of his potential path in this lifetime. However, since Pluto is in the house of his subconscious mind and in Libra, he may have had problems with authority and the legal system that affects him on a deep level.

The twelfth house relates to the subconscious mind, and always suggests something from the past. However, despite this, the subconscious is now helping him in a career, which again blends personal values and higher consciousness with drive based on his foundational values in the present, as legal counsel for a very strong union. Darius is living his chart and overcoming the ADD/ADHD.

His Ascendant is the midpoint between Mars in the eleventh house in Virgo (perhaps suggesting he was a warrior or in a very aggressive group), and Uranus in the first house, which can mean personal chaos. Uranus is retrograde, and can be relating to past conditions. In Scorpio, perhaps this involved clandestine matters. Was he a spy who was caught? **The Ascendant midpoint of his**

Mars and Uranus suggests the ADD/ADHD.

The true tell, however, is Hidalgo, at 11 Libra 53 in the twelfth house of subconscious matters and conjunct North Node. **Hidalgo is also widely conjunct Pluto in Libra, and all three are in the twelfth house.** This is the house where past conditions are deeply buried in the subconscious, but opposite the sixth house of health, suggesting a physical manifestation of the twelfth house condition. In other words, this goes beyond the phobia stage and into the physical. This is further reinforced by the South Node in the sixth house suggesting past conditions affecting health. Since the South Node is ruled by Mars in the eleventh house of groups and since Mars (suggesting the warrior) is in Virgo, all of this can tie into what the Hidalgo might mean for Darius this time around. In the past he may well have experienced an extreme event as a martyr! With Mars here, I think possibly he was a military martyr.

Hidalgo alone, with Pluto and the North Node, all three all in the twelfth house, is a pretty strong indication of a person who could have ADD/ADHD. When the twelfth house placements combine with the first house Uranus opposite Chiron, you can see a strong indication of hyperactivity or the ADHD. Even though the placements of ADD and ADHD are pretty much the same, there are times when hyperactivity is strongly suggested.

Neptune retrograde in Sagittarius in the third house of conscious mind brings in past conditions. With the sign of Sagittarius, higher consciousness, religion and philosophy are also suggested, along with past conditions of higher consciousness activity. There is a lack of clarity with Neptune, which could relate to ADD/ADHD, as well.

Looking again at Darius' retrograde planets, the retrograde Uranus is innately a rebel and since this is in his first house, it represents his personality. This also means he was likely rebellious in the past, and he may now be paying for this. He will change, jump from one thing to another on a deep level with no conscious rationale. It's a rather a tough place for a retrograde Uranus. He either lives outside societal norms or at the very least, they don't matter to him. This may be a highly spiritual placement, but at the same time perhaps seeking the depths of human psyche and physical experience. Also, his is an innately psychic placement of the first order.

Neptune is retrograde in the third house of conscious mind. Even without other placements this often suggests ADD/ADHD. It is in Sagittarius so again, he probably was in trouble for higher ideals and now his conscious mind reacts in a defensive manner with the ADD/ADHD. This is a highly psychic placement, as well. He will talk in circles or go about getting to the point by almost stream of conscious conversations, an ADD/ADHD type of speaking. He almost communicates better with actions or non-verbal methods (again psychically). He is innately a dreamer and may tend to take the problems of all around him and consciously feel their pain.

In Sagittarius he is a truth seeker and great humanitarian, and this goes to the depth of his being. He would be a great teacher even with the ADD/ADHD. It is interesting that his two retrograde planets are both those associated with the ADD/ADHD. Even without other placements this often suggests ADD/ADHD.

It is interesting to note that Darius' Ceres is 15 Capricorn 17, retrograde in the third house, so it appears he was verbal and communicative in past lives in a nurturing manner, but in Capricorn, on a down-to-earth level, and opposite Jupiter in the tenth house, so it was expansive and very public. Jupiter is in the astrological sign of Cancer which suggests a nurturer as well. Past life communication to help others in a public forum.

Now we look at Ceres retrograde which is square Pluto in Libra in the twelfth house of hidden conditions with Pluto reformation qualities, as well as Ceres square both his Ascendant and Eris in the sixth house of healing. Also Pluto sits with Hidalgo in this twelfth house. Eris sits in the house of health and healing along with karmic South Node. There is little doubt that Ceres relationship to the planets discussed was a tremendous influence on what was done in the past and what is being done in this lifetime. Darius was and is the nurturer (a labor attorney), helping others and trying to heal wrongs, and the twelfth house placements reinforce the karmic conditions.

Hidalgo, at 3 Libra 53 in Darius' twelfth house, suggests a deep rooted sense of justice, which is part of his being even though he may be unaware of the trauma that creates this feeling, and of which feelings are also expressed with his retrograde planets.

Hidalgo is the midpoint of his Jupiter at 19 Cancer in the tenth house, and Neptune retrograde at 15 Sagittarius in the third house. This is telling in and of itself. It is also the midpoint of Mars at 18 Virgo in the eleventh house and Ascendant at 16 Libra. This, again, suggests ramifications of the warrior for a noble cause. Hidalgo is also at the midpoint of Sun at 23 Cancer and again, Neptune. I may use a bit larger orb for this midpoint, since it is tied to a retrograde planet, plus his tenth house Sun and Jupiter.

Though I usually use only a one degree conjunction for midpoint configurations, there are times when you can see how strong the meaning of the combination might be when you also consider 2 or 3 degrees of orb. It depends on whether the planets are retrograde and what they represent within the chart, in relationship to the person's life.

BETTY

Betty, (whose chart is on page 43) was born January 24, 1939, at 4:35 am in Long Beach, California. She is an astrologer.

Betty has a T-square with the Midheaven at 14 Libra, Mercury at 17 Capricorn in the first house and Saturn at 12 Aries in the third house. This suggests obstacles in her personal thought processes, since Mercury or thought and communication is in her personal first house, while Saturn, the planet of obstacles and karma, is in her third house of communication. This will affect her career as well. Taken alone, this would not suggest ADD or ADHD, but it is a factor that enhances other placements.

She has a yod (or "finger of fate" aspect) with Midheaven at 14 Libra (ruled by Venus in the twelfth house in Sagittarius), Moon at 16 Pisces in the third house and Uranus at 13 Taurus in her fifth house of creativity. Uranus and Moon point toward her Midheaven.

With Moon in Pisces, Betty is highly intuitive and Uranus in the fifth house suggests chaos, but also a lot of energy for creativity or working with children. Both point toward her Midheaven, suggesting areas of work that would fulfill her. Midheaven is 14 Libra and is ruled by Venus in the twelfth house of subconscious mind.

Venus is in Sagittarius, suggesting that her subconscious is deeply affected by higher consciousness and religion, etc. This is the first indication that a higher moral standard may exist on an unconscious level. Again, this alone would not suggest the martyr that is often suggested in ADD/ADHD placements, but it does enhance those placements. People with ADD/ADHD are very good at working with children, who also must switch from one thing to another or they are bored out of their minds. Thus, Betty's yod is a perfect placement for an educator.

Her South Node is conjunct Uranus by degree in the fifth house, indicating the generational influence in her past life and combined with Uranus, a lot of chaos is suggested.

More importantly, the South Node is the midpoint (2 degrees) of Chiron which is retrograde in Cancer and Saturn in the third house of thought and communication. Here is a strong indication of a place needing healing (Chiron retrograde is karmic and is also foundational, since it is Cancer). Moon is in Pisces in the third house, indicating fluctuating mind patterns. Moon in Pisces in the third house is also highly intuitive, but is one who also thinks of problems of others and may not be able to distinguish between what is real and unreal, at times. This is a placement that must always watch prescriptions and mind altering items, and is also a pretty strong indicator of ADD or ADHD.

An even stronger indicator is that Chiron is the midpoint between Saturn in Aries (bringing in obstacles and karma) in the third house of communication and Neptune in Virgo in the Ninth House of higher consciousness. Neptune is retrograde, so it appears that communication and thought are in need of healing due to past events of a ninth house nature. Since Neptune is retrograde this may mean either a religious person or perhaps an educator who tried to help others, but paid the price for that in the past, and is now, in this present life, defending herself with ADD or ADHD.

Pluto is retrograde at 0 degrees Leo and is the midpoint of

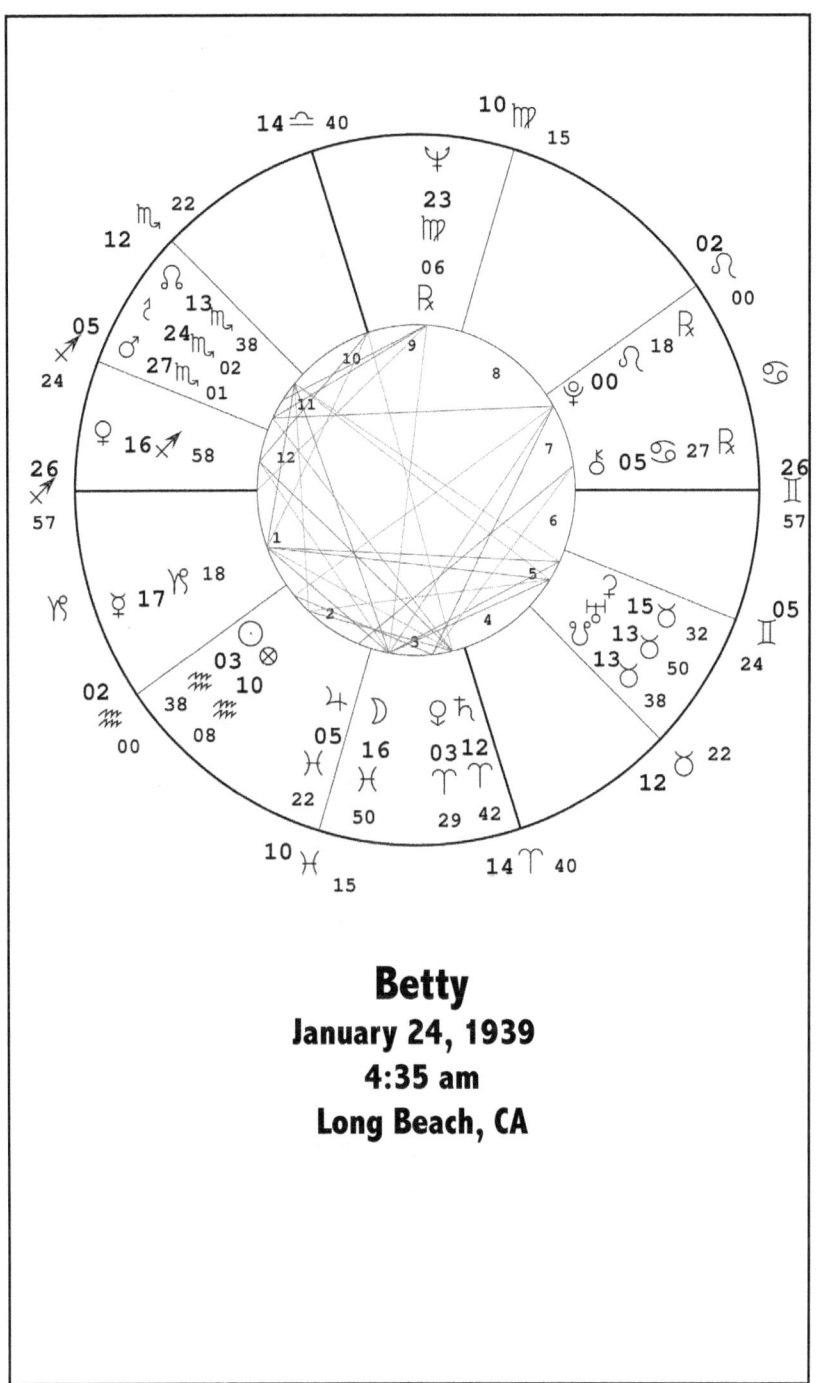

Betty
January 24, 1939
4:35 am
Long Beach, CA

Uranus in the fifth house at 13 degrees Taurus and the Midheaven which is 14 Libra. Pluto retrograde, is of course, karmic and Pluto is generational. As a midpoint between chaotic Uranus in the fifth house of creativity and Midheaven, there is some indication of perhaps an actor or athlete or someone in the spotlight actually using a public career to shed light on a situation—but with Uranus, of course, there is chaos and unpredictability. In and of itself, this placement is a reinforcement of ADD/ADHD placements. Pluto is the reformer or suggestive of power struggles, so the reforming nature of a martyr may be involved.

Another reinforcement of ADD/ADHD is Mercury in the first house, which is at the midpoint of Mars in the eleventh house in Scorpio and Jupiter in Pisces in the second house. Again, this is not necessarily the placement of ADD/ADHD, but reinforces the placement.

Each reinforcement placement makes the ADD/ADHD placements stronger, and this chart has quite a bit of reinforcement placements. Here Mercury, which is the mind and how it works is in Capricorn, which seems like it would be very pragmatic. But, Mercury as a midpoint between Mars in Scorpio in the eleventh house of groups (a warrior, to generational themes now) and Jupiter in Pisces, which is an expansion of Piscean traits such as intuition, but also of deception or self-deception, and of taking on the world's problems, especially with the ruler of Pisces in the ninth house and retrograde, is more complex. For example, past conditions of higher consciousness, religion, etc., come into play with Jupiter in the second house of values.

In all this you can see a kind of circling motion, around what could be a practical mind, with higher ideals and extreme intuition, fighting for a group with some kind of karma involved. It sounds quite a bit like one who would be a martyr.

Saturn, which is totally karmic in the third house, showing obstacles in thought and learning, is also reinforced by the midpoint configuration of Mercury on Mars/Jupiter. This is reinforced to an even greater extent by the Moon in Pisces in the third house (very psychic, such that she probably knows why she has ADD today). Again, Moon as the midpoint between Mercury and

Uranus in the fifth house, indicates the chaos of Uranus to the conscious mind.

A true ADD placement, not just a reinforcement, is Chiron retrograde (indicating very past conditions or a place in need of healing) at the midpoint between Saturn in the third house and Neptune in the Ninth House. Here we bring in three strong factors of Ninth House values, with conscious mental obstacles and the need of healing. We have a true relationship between planets and Chiron that can suggest ADD/ADHD. Also, Chiron in Cancer is ruled by the Moon is in the third house of conscious mind, and Moon is in Pisces, ruled by Neptune in the ninth house. With both Neptune and Chiron retrograde, the implications of ADD/ADHD are quite strong. This placement also suggests marriage or partnership issues that will be repeated until the cycle is broken—but that is an aside.

In fact, Pluto retrograde in Leo suggests an overt attempt to deconstruct the powers that be and, this is what Betty was in trouble for in the past. This placement creates a very strong suggestion of ADD/ADHD, especially when considered along with the midpoints discussed and Neptune retrograde in the ninth house.

Eris is in the third house of communication and square Chiron, which is retrograde, so it appears there is a karmic point of healing that may affect communication now, and there was a transformational component, as well.

Perhaps the most important indicator of the ADD/ADHD is the placement of Hidalgo in the eleventh house of groups conjunct Mars in Scorpio. Hidalgo conjunct Mars suggests the violence, while Scorpio suggests clandestine activity (perhaps a group, since it's the eleventh house) and Pluto, retrograde in Leo, rules Scorpio. All together this suggests a deconstruction of the powers that be, and together this strongly indicates someone who was in trouble in the past for activities. Also, with Neptune retrograde in the ninth house, the person was someone of higher education, such as a priest or a professor working for good of others on a very grounded level (Neptune in Virgo). This is the true placement that is reinforced by the other placements already discussed.

Even though Mars is not retrograde, it is also heavily associated with placements of past life conditions, and conjunct Hidalgo in Betty's chart, it is very heavily associated with this asteroid and what it represents, thus taking on the karmic aura of the martyr. Any planet that is conjunct Hidalgo will bring in past conditions that are associated with the Hidalgo theme.

With Neptune in the ninth house and retrograde, Betty is trying again in this life to teach the world what is important to her, while at the same time, she may take on the problems of others, or at least feel their problems as if they were her own. She is highly sensitive to people. At the same time, she is trying to find out what is right for her while keeping herself safe, by using the ADD/ADHD as a defense. What is in the past is often her felt reality in the present, so with ADD/ADHD, she is trying not to experience it again.

It is interesting to note that Ceres at 15 Taurus is opposite the Hidalgo placement by a wide orb, and the nurturing influence of Ceres may come into play, as well.

CARRIE

Carrie was born April 13, 1932 in New England, ND. (See her chart on the next page.) She was a county employee, is now the mother of eight, the stepmother of three and a grandmother.

Carrie does not know her birth time. The use of 12:00 noon to study a chart for which there is no known birth time is a long standing practice of astrologers. This noon time works very well for ADD/ADHD placements, especially since it is the relationship between the planets themselves that is the most important. I have found this with virtually all ADD/ADHD charts for which I have no birth time.

What jumps out at me first in Carrie's chart is that she has a stellium of planets in Aries, that includes by a wide out-of-sign conjunction to the North Node in Pisces. Mars, Mercury, Uranus and Sun are all in Aries and Mercury is retrograde, so past conditions come into play. With Uranus in the stellium in close

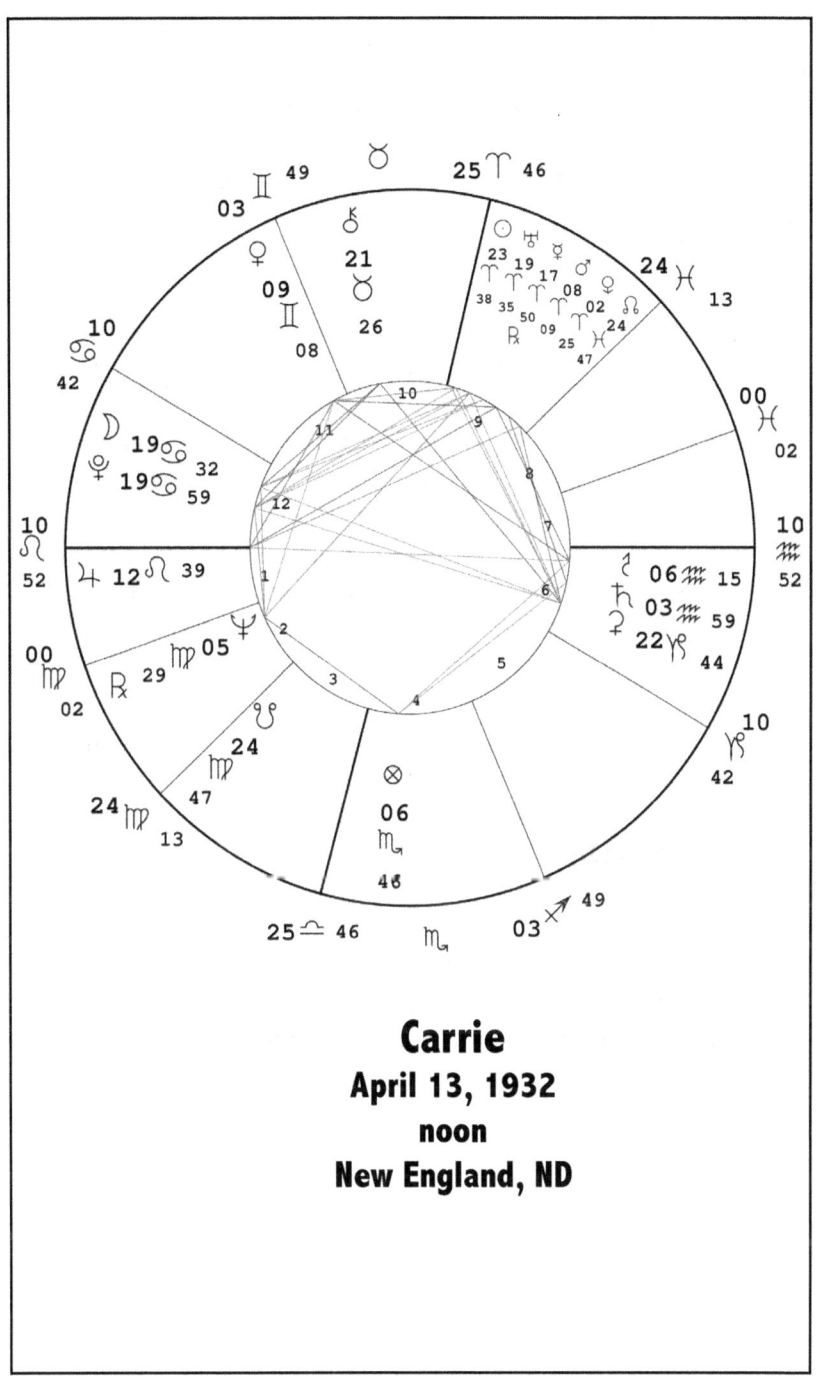

Carrie
April 13, 1932
noon
New England, ND

ADD and ADHD Placements

conjunction to Mercury, we can also see chaos of the mind. Since these planets are in Aries, she has energy, but her mind is going from one thing to another rapidly. This is a strong indication of ADD/ADHD. Eris is conjunct Mars in this stellium, as well. With this conjunction and the Uranus-Mercury retrograde conjunction, we are getting shades of transformation, too. Additionally, Eris is quincunx Neptune in Virgo.

Hidalgo is in Aquarius, which is ruled by chaotic Uranus, suggesting the ADD/ADHD, and Uranus is conjunct Mercury, so it will affect her mind and its processes. Hidalgo's sign is in a square relationship to Chiron in Taurus. Since Chiron, shows a place that needs healing, we have an indicator of ADD/ADHD. Hidalgo is also conjunct Saturn, which brings in past karma. I think that Carrie's past life troubles may have been related to some new technology or far reaching inventions that threatened the powers that be, and that may have caused past life trouble.

Hidalgo is quincunx Pluto in Cancer which also may indicate the ADD/ADHD, if there are other strong ADD/ADHD placements.

Another strong indication of ADD/ADHD is Uranus in Aries to the exact degree square Pluto in Cancer with Mercury retrograde also square. Here we have the mind, chaos, reformation and power struggles, with the past brought in by the retrograde Mercury. This is a recipe for ADD/ADHD.

Saturn is also square by a slightly wide orb (5 degrees) to Mars. This may imply a physical battle that is partially causing the ADD/ADHD. Remember, though, that Saturn is karmic and does not have to be retrograde to figure into a possible past life interpretation. Still, it seems to me that anytime a retrograde planet is part of an aspect pattern, is more likely to signal the karma that is related to the ADD/ADHD.

As you can see, even without a time of birth, the ADD/ADHD placements are apparent. The delineation of Carrie's placements is somewhat shorter than with other charts viewed because I do not have a birth time. Her example is to demonstrate that we do not need a birth time to see the relationship between the planets and Hidalgo. The only item not covered is the Moon which although significant is not necessarily crucial to ADD/ADHD delineation We will see this in a celebrity chart in the next chapter as well.

DECLAN

Declan (whose chart is on page 53) was born January 23, 1945 in Long Beach, CA, at 5:55 PM. He has a Ph.D. in Education.

He went to public school prior to the wide spread treatment for ADD/ADHD, and saw his school records on his teacher's desk. He read that he was passed along because he was "not a problem."

Later, he joined the army and became a black belt in karate. He found Karate helped him concentrate, and I feel army discipline was probably a big help to him as well. He is now on medication for his ADD/ADHD, and is doing wonderfully well.

Planetary placements indicating Declan's ADD/ADHD are apparent. His Hidalgo is 11 Capricorn in his sixth house of health and conjunct Mercury, suggesting a health issue with mental activities and communication. Mars is also conjunct Hidalgo, as is Mercury which suggests a lot of energy, but also that his thoughts could be rapidly going from one thing to another.

Also Hidalgo is conjunct (by a wide orb) his South Node or his past lives. With Mars in Capricorn, I think his past humanitarian martyrdom was probably connected to military activity for a humane cause (much like Hidalgo himself). This suggests a lot of energy put into a lot of very hard work.

All of the planets in Declan's sixth house are ruled by Saturn, which is retrograde in his twelfth house. Saturn is in Cancer, so his foundational values are deeply embedded in his subconscious, stemming from past life activities for which he got into trouble big time. Saturn is of course very karmic and it is retrograde, so it is even more karmic. This affects his subconscious, and by rulership also his mental health, since Mercury is in the sixth house.

Mercury and Mars conjunct Hidalgo in the sixth house is indicative of the ADD/ADHD, and with the ruler of Capricorn, Saturn, in the twelfth house of subconscious, the suggestions of ADD/ADHD are even stronger. Hidalgo's manifestations are very deeply embedded into Declan's being. His North Node is in his twelfth house, suggesting that he now must balance his subconscious inhibitions so that he can overcome his health issues or the ADD/ADHD. His foundational values, since Saturn and the North Node are in Cancer, come from a deep, subconscious place as well. He is in a position to repeat past actions and must take care that he does not do so.

All of the planets in his sixth house of work are ruled by Saturn which is retrograde in his twelfth house. Saturn is in Cancer so his foundational values are deeply embedded in his subconscious, stemming from past life activities for which he got into trouble—big time!

Saturn is, of course, very karmic and it is retrograde, so it deeply affects Declan's subconscious, and by rulership, also his mental health, as shown by Mercury in the sixth house. Mercury and Mars conjunct Hidalgo in the sixth house is also indicative of the ADD/ADHD, especially with the ruler of Capricorn, Saturn, in the twelfth house of the subconscious. This makes other suggestions of ADD/ADHD even stronger.

Hidalgo's manifestations are very deeply embedded into Declan's being. His North Node is in his twelfth house, suggesting that he now must balance his subconscious inhibitions, so that he can overcome his health issues or the ADD/ADHD. His foundational values (since Saturn and the North Node are in Cancer) come from a deep, subconscious place, as well. Again, he is in a position to repeat past actions and must take care that he does not do so.

Another interesting fact is that he has Sagittarius on the cusp on his sixth house at the critical 29 degrees. The 29th degree suggests that he may not use the energy as well as he should. Sagittarius is the natural ruler of the ninth house, suggesting his health problems are based in part on his higher consciousness. With Hidalgo in the sixth house, this again suggests that his health problems are based on past life activities as a martyr. The combination of his sixth house planets and Hidalgo with their rulership in the twelfth house, where his karmic Saturn retrograde resides, along with the cusp of the sixth house in Sagittarius (higher philosophy and religion), all add up to strong ADD/

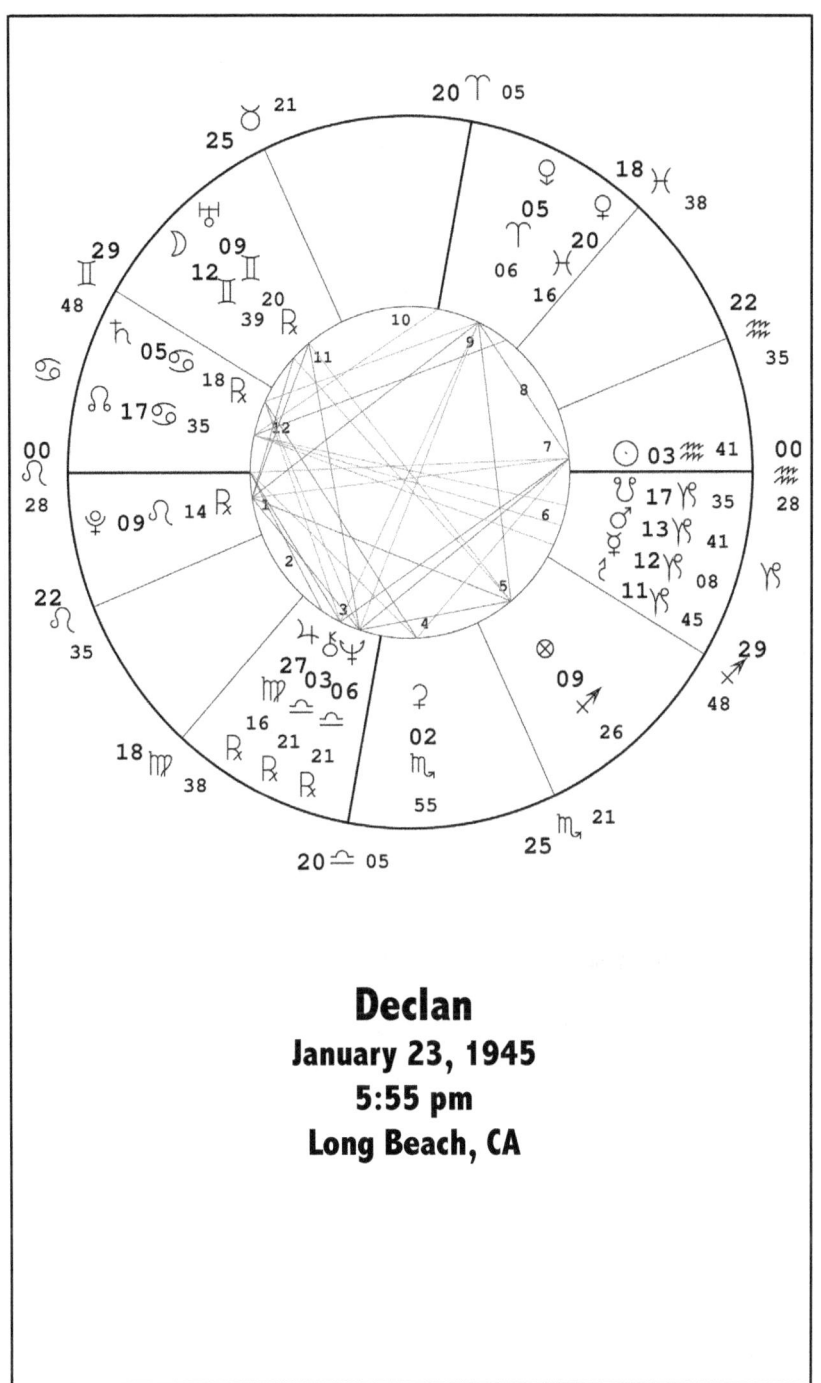

Declan
January 23, 1945
5:55 pm
Long Beach, CA

ADHD placements.

Mercury conjunct Mars suggests a lot of mental activity, communication and perhaps a lot of mental tension.

Hidalgo is contraparallel (an aspect similar to an opposition) to Pluto in the first house, and Pluto is retrograde. This suggests a reformer who is perhaps vying for power. This fits with the martyr type of person. Obviously, the power struggle was for a cause and not for personal gain, as suggested by his other placements. Pluto in Leo suggests he was quite prominent or a public figure in the fight.

Hidalgo is also contraparallel or opposite Saturn in the twelfth house. Since Saturn is a planet of great karma and sits in the twelfth house of subconscious, Declan's Hidalgo issues are very deeply buried, which can lead to the ADD/ADHD. Taken one step further, Cancer is ruled by the Moon which is in the eleventh house in Gemini and conjunct Uranus in Gemini.

Uranus and the Moon in the eleventh house of groups, tied by the contraparallel to Saturn retrograde with its heavy karma in the Twelfth house, together suggest that communication or written activities of a group in a past life or lives may be causing the chaos of the mind (Gemini) in his current life. In fact, almost his entire chart ties into to this idea.

Uranus is also retrograde, so there is a lot of karma involved. Uranus in Gemini, alone, suggests a mind that is chaotic. Hidalgo is quincunx Uranus, as well, contributing to the ADD/ADHD even further. Also, Mercury in the sixth house rules Uranus in Gemini, so again we have health, the mind and chaos.

If you look at Declan's third house of communication, Jupiter is retrograde in Virgo, Chiron is retrograde in Libra and Neptune is retrograde in Libra. That is a tough third house, even without the Hidalgo placement conjunct Mercury, natural ruler of the third house. With Jupiter, Chiron and Neptune in the third house, he has a tremendous insightful mind which may take on the problems of others, but may also need drugs to help the mind heal. Since all of these planets are retrograde, his entire conscious mind and mental activity would be influenced by past life events.

Even without such strong Hidalgo influence, he may have

had trouble concentrating, with his imagination going wild. Hidalgo just pushes this third house toward the ADD/ADHD. He should beware of narcotics with his retrograde Neptune in the third house in Libra. His mind wants balance. Also, his high degree of intuition and escapism are factors to be considered. Prescription medications, alone, must be watched, let alone any other forms of escapism. With his third house, self medicating in early years could have been a problem.

Another outlet for Declan would be imaginative creativity. With his retrograde Neptune combined with his Part of Fortune in the fifth house of creativity in Sagittarius, his form of creativity would be based on his higher consciousness or higher ideals. It appears that everything he does is based on deep and often past life foundational values. He works for the good of the underdog as much as possible, and he definitely wants to help others.

The sign of Capricorn in the sixth house suggests a need for work that requires discipline and responsibility. Taken with the entire chart, especially his South Node in the sixth house, this suggests that he might have been a military man in a past life who was a prisoner of war, or in some way, may have had a violent end while fighting for his values. He also may have been a war correspondent or a photographer who reached the same kind of end, and that could be why the military appealed to him in this lifetime.

Leo is the showman of the zodiac and Pluto is retrograde in Leo in the first house. This suggests that, personally, Declan was prominent at one point in time, and that his prominence was probably as a reformer. Since Pluto is quincunx Mercury, and Hidalgo and Mars are in his sixth house, there was an effect on his person and on his health. It is interesting to note that Declan has five planets retrograde, as well as Chiron (and also the Nodes which are always retrograde and karmic, anyway). There are a lot of past conditions with which Declan is dealing.

Uranus retrograde in Gemini and conjunct the Moon in Gemini indicates erratic thought processes, as well as unusual thoughts, changes or fluctuations of the mind. Again, this reinforces the indicators of ADD/ADHD.

His strength, seen from where the Sun is located in the

chart, is in the seventh house, so he is good as a partner. That his Sun is in Aquarius suggests he is also good with technology and anything that will advance society. The Sun is conjunct the cusp of this seventh house, his Descendant, so is opposite the cusp of his first house, Ascendant. He may look to partnerships to help with his personal being, and in all of that, he must find a balance.

Mercury is at the midpoint between Hidalgo and Mars in the sixth house and is also part of a stellium in that house. This alone indicates ADD/ADHD tendencies. Another midpoint that may influence ADD/ADHD is Pluto retrograde in the first house at the midpoint between Moon in Gemini (representing fluctuation of the mind) and Neptune in the third house of the conscious mind. Pluto is in the first house, so this is a personal placement for Declan. Pluto retrograde suggests a previous lifetime reformer or a person in a power struggle, so this brings in the karma.

The two newly named planets of Ceres and Eris also play a role in Declan's ADD/ADHD placements. Ceres is at 2 Scorpio in his fourth house and is trine Saturn retrograde in Cancer in the twelfth house. This is very much the nurturer helping with past karmic conditions to the extreme with Saturn retrograde and since Saturn is in Cancer, you are getting a double dose of nurturing. This should help with the karmic ramifications that suggest the ADD/ADHD.

On the other hand, Eris and its transformational qualities also may have an affect on the ADD/ADHD in a more Plutonian way. Eris is at 5 Aries in the ninth house of higher consciousness so you see a tendency to still want to transform higher consciousness. It is square Hidalgo in the sixth house suggesting difficulty with health due to Hidalgo's manifestations. This can be ADD/ADHD. It is also square Saturn retrograde. Saturn retrograde is very karmic, both Eris and Pluto suggest difficulty and obstacles in transformation. Saturn may include group activity, since it is in the eleventh house. Eris in Aries should give Declan a leg up on these tendencies this time around.

With all of this difficulty, Declan's placements indicate an intuitive person and this is why he was able to do things as a young man that would help his ADD/ADHD.

Often, sports or extreme discipline such as the military help with ADD/ADHD. Also, working with children is a great profession for those with ADD, since children have to bounce from one thing to another. Declan most likely intuitively gravitated to all three—the military (which was natural from past lives), sports or Karate and also elementary education. He self-medicated himself by his actions long before the diagnosis of ADD/ADHD. This is a person working out his astrology chart in a positive way, even though he is a poster boy for ADD/ADHD.

NATHANIEL

Nathaniel ("Nate"), who is the son of Declan, was born February 28, 1986, at 4:19 A.M. in Pirmasens, Germany. He graduated from college and then joined the peace corps. See page 59 for his chart.

Yes, there is a genetic component to this entire study. Again, we choose how, who and when we come back (karmically). We choose the genetics, often because family can relate to the same problems we incur. As I said, this is karmic, but it is also buried in the physical. It is not just a phobia.

Nate's chart is a good example of the use of midpoints pointing toward ADD or ADHD. Nate has Mars at 14 Sagittarius in the eleventh house (the derivative twelfth house from the twelfth house). Mars is conjunct his Saturn/Uranus midpoint, with Saturn in the eleventh house and Uranus in the actual twelfth house. This strong direct midpoint (involving both derivative and actual houses) shows a lot of subconscious restriction and chaos coupled with Mars energy, all suggesting ADD/ADHD. This is a very heavy combination.

Saturn, a planet of Karma, is in Sagittarius, suggesting karma is tied to his higher consciousness. Mars is tied to action, based on his higher consciousness and Uranus in the twelfth house suggests that something traumatic may be causing unusual reaction or chaos that is based in higher consciousness. This is very much a placement that could indicate a past life as a martyr who worked with a group or society for a worthy cause and perhaps clandestinely.

Saturn's placement in relationship to the other planets is what indicates the karma. The sign of Sagittarius is what brings in his higher consciousness, ideals, and perhaps is suggesting that he may have been (or could be) a professor or a priest. Although the planets themselves are not retrograde, their relationship to the karmic Saturn is what creates this karmic situation, along with Uranus in the twelfth house of the subconscious mind. Uranus in the twelfth house, alone, brings in a lot of subconscious chaos.

The Sun, Mars and Saturn in Sagittarius and Chiron in Gemini form a T-square, with the Sun at the midpoint between Saturn and Chiron, to the exact degree. This brings in, along with Saturian karma, the second house of values. With Sun in the second house and Chiron in Gemini, thought processes in need of healing are suggested. This is quite indicative of ADD/ADHD.

Since Chiron is in Nathaniel's fifth house of creativity, sports and the discipline of art or music will be of benefit to him. Gemini, is his second house of values, and the Gemini ruler, Mercury is here, so he will need to do something of value to himself creatively. This will help him a lot with his ADD/ADHD.

Nate's Sun is in Pisces, indicating a great sense of imagination, and he is also a very intuitive person. He knows what people are about and that probably reinforces his subconscious need to keep his thoughts to himself, or his desire to mask his intelligence and communication with the ADD/ADHD. He also has a stellium of planets in his second house of values—Jupiter, Sun, Venus and Mercury. He will want to only put his energy and extreme intuition into projects that are important to his higher value system. Although the Sun is here, and he will be able to acquire wealth, but with his planets in Pisces, the wealth will not be as important as the things that his heart tells him are good for everyone. He has a very strong intuition which breaks through into his consciousness. He chooses when not to express himself with his ADD/ADHD defense mechanism.

His Ascendant is conjunct Hidalgo, with only one degree of orb. His Hidalgo is still in the twelfth house, though, so his martyrdom is buried very deeply in his subconscious, manifesting in an actual physical malady. Both Hidalgo and the Ascendant are

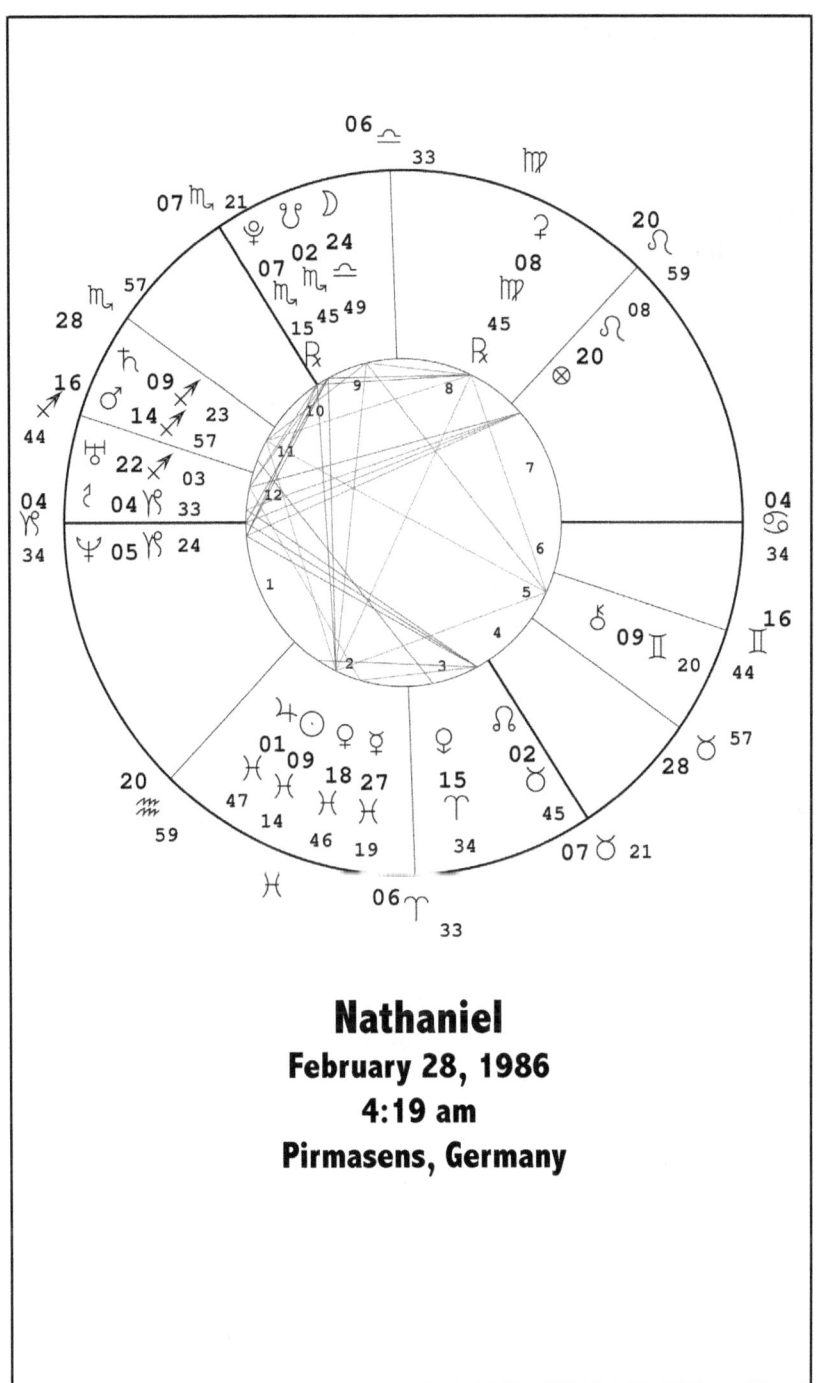

Nathaniel
February 28, 1986
4:19 am
Pirmasens, Germany

Three Celebrities with ADD/ADHD

in Capricorn ruled by that eleventh house Saturn, so we now have Saturn and Hidalgo linked again. How much more karmic can it get?

Hidalgo is in his twelfth house of hidden activities and subconscious mind, but also of institutions such as prison. We are seeing a subconscious dealing with Uranus in Sagittarius, or chaos stemming from a belief system, and perhaps prison or worse.

Still, Hidalgo is so very close to the first house (technically in house 12, but in a one degree conjunction to Ascendant), Nate cannot help but be personally affected by this placement. Hidalgo is also quincunx (by a wide orb) to his Chiron in Gemini. ADD/ADHD, or a need for healing within mental activity, can be strongly indicated with Chiron in Gemini, especially with a connection to the martyr asteroid. Hidalgo is also conjunct Neptune in the first house. With Hidalgo in the twelfth house and these aspects, Nathaniel may have dreams of past life conditions that could be pretty scary.

Nate's Eris at 15 Aries in the third house of communication is square his Hidalgo in the twelfth house. Here we have a transformational planet square Hidalgo–the catalyst for ADD/ADHD planets—in the twelfth house of hidden activities and also institutions. Aggressive communication is square Hidalgo in the house of hidden matters and thus seems like a karmic condition to me. Eris is trine Mars in Sagittarius in the eleventh house and it appears as though he may repeat the pattern of speaking out perhaps in group settings but very aggressively with Mars. This is an easy flow of energy for him and should be a caution in light of the Eris/Hidalgo placements. Eris is also square Capricorn and thus square Neptune in the first house. He will again take on feelings of others with regard to earthly, hard matters and speak. He is personally very intuitive as to what others may need.

On the other hand Ceres is retrograde at 8 Virgo in the eighth house. Ceres is karmic so the nurturing feelings he has come from past times and are very deeply ingrained into his subconscious. This placement is sextile Pluto retrograde in Scorpio in his ninth house. Here we have a totally karmic placement. The nurturer and the religious figure or professor and the like are represented by a sextile, so he will have an easy flow of energy to repeat the same patterns that may have gotten him into trouble in the past, but he also has the safety net of nurturing Ceres. Ceres is square karmic Saturn at 9 degrees Sagittarius in the eleventh house of groups and in Sagittarius, this would be groups that are working now, or have worked in the past, for Sagittarian ideals. He keeps repeating this theme over and over. He works with groups again and again.

Ceres is also square Chiron in Gemini in the fifth house. Ceres retrograde square Chiron in the sign that rules the mind and communication indicates someone who in the past acted in a nurturing manner and feels this need to help heal again—this is his comfort zone. However, with all of the other karmic placements, it appears that he may well have been in trouble in the past for this same type of work, and in his present life, he may be repeating the past.

Neptune is sextile Pluto retrograde in the ninth house of higher consciousness, indicating that he may repeat his humane activities, but there may also be power struggles involved. Still, he innately feels that he must help.

This brings me to Pluto retrograde in the ninth house. Pluto is generational, suggests power and control issues, and is in his ninth house of higher consciousness—past and perhaps present. This is a very strong indication of someone like Hidalgo, who fought for rights, but perhaps in Nathaniel's past life, he did this on foreign soil. If so, it is interesting that Nate is repeating this pattern by joining the peace corps, and is now in a country where society has been repressed. It is a very spiritual society. He loves it!

The Jupiter/Pluto midpoint is conjunct Nate's Ascendant with Jupiter in his second house of values and Pluto in his ninth house of higher ideals and religion. This reinforces his current attitude of reformation while defending himself with his ADD/ADHD. Hidalgo is also at this midpoint, suggesting the past martyr who is ready to do it again.

In fact the South Node in the ninth house also suggests one who is coming from a place of religion or higher learning, and the North Node in his third house suggests that he must learn to balance this with his communication skills, the skills that he may be trying to avoid with the ADD/ADHD. This can be very tough, indeed.

Nate also has a Thor's hammer with Chiron square the Sun and sesquiquadrate both Pluto and Saturn. Sun is within his second house of values in Pisces (his unconscious mind coupled with tremendous insight greatly affects his values), Chiron is in Gemini in the fifth house, indicating a place needing healing, and Pluto is retrograde in Scorpio in his ninth house of higher philosophy/religion and foreign matters—the need for balance and justice. The Ninth house is the house of Sagittarius. This brings in his peace corps activity now. Remember, Thor's hammer is a gift from God but only for the brave.

Again, with his retrograde Pluto and the South Node in the ninth house, he probably will repeat his past conditions of trying to help others, based on his own higher consciousness. Since both Pluto and South Node are in Scorpio, perhaps a lot of his past activities were investigative or clandestine. Scorpio is the natural ruler of the eighth house which, among other things, brings in investigations and endings. He was more than likely a religious martyr in a past life, or a person who was murdered for somehow trying to improve life for humanity.

I brought actual past life experience into my delineation of ADD/ADHD of the last two gentlemen discussed, since I know both of them and also know that they do not mind my being this specific with their charts. The other examples fall much into the same category as a martyr but I have only stated what their past activities may have involved.

CHAPTER 4

THREE CELEBRITIES WITH ADD/ADHD

I am including the natal charts of three celebrities, that I have confirmed via the news media including personal interviews on television, who have either ADD or ADHD. The following three charts are very interesting examples. I have included the chart of a famous athlete, a famous singer/songwriter and a famous actor/comedienne. I have the birth time for two of the three charts and again used a 12:00 noon for the third chart which fits very well. Since the relationship between the planets is so important, you will see the ADD/ADHD connection without rectification of the third chart.

I have not gone into quite as much detail as in the previous charts from chapter 3, since patterns indicating ADD/ADHD are repetitious and it is the repeated themes that suggest ADD/ADHD. You will recognize the placements quite easily.

STEVEN TYLER

Steven Tyler (whose chart is on page 65), was born March 26, 1948 at 11:18 pm in Yonkers, New York. He is the lead singer and songwriter for Aerosmith. Since he is well known, I am going to look at a few indicators of his fame and then the ADD/ADHD placements.

Steven has Neptune in the 10th house of fame, so something in the arts and using his intuitive imagination is indicated. Since it is in Libra, this will help him keep a balance, or help balance, the ADD/ADHD. His Sun in Aries indicates a lot of drive. More importantly, his Pluto conjunct Saturn and Mars are all in Leo, the actor/showman, and all three placements are retrograde, so his entertainment ability is karmic—he has been here before and he wants to be here again. This is his comfort zone. Remember, your comfort zone is what you have done in the past. He has Venus in Taurus in the sixth house, indicating that he will work for comfort. He has a love of luxury and intends to get it. He will be over indulgent. This may affect his health, and his work may suffer as well. His Pluto in Leo is also the exact midpoint between his sixth house Venus in Taurus and his Moon in the eleventh house in Scorpio. He will instinctively know how to be famous.

Now the ADD/ADHD

Steven Tyler's Hidalgo is in the fourth house of his foundation and also the end of matters. At 26 Pisces 14, Hidalgo is still conjunct the 24 Pisces 12 cusp of his fourth house close to his third house of his mind. This conjunction with Hidalgo just within the fourth house indicates that the effects of Hidalgo are part of the foundation of his being, but also closely relate to his mental activity.

Hidalgo sextiles Venus in the sixth house of work, and the Piscean intuition of his Hidalgo combined with Venus brings forth work that will give him the fame he almost needs. Hidalgo is also trine Chiron in Scorpio in the twelfth house of hidden conditions and the subconscious mind.

Thus, Chiron—a place that needs healing—is trine Hidalgo in Pisces, which is the natural sign of the twelfth house. His mind, on a deep level needs healing; however this placement will actually help him deal with the ADD/ADHD.

Ceres is at 19 Taurus in the sixth house and is opposite the karmic South Node at 16 Scorpio in the eleventh house. This means

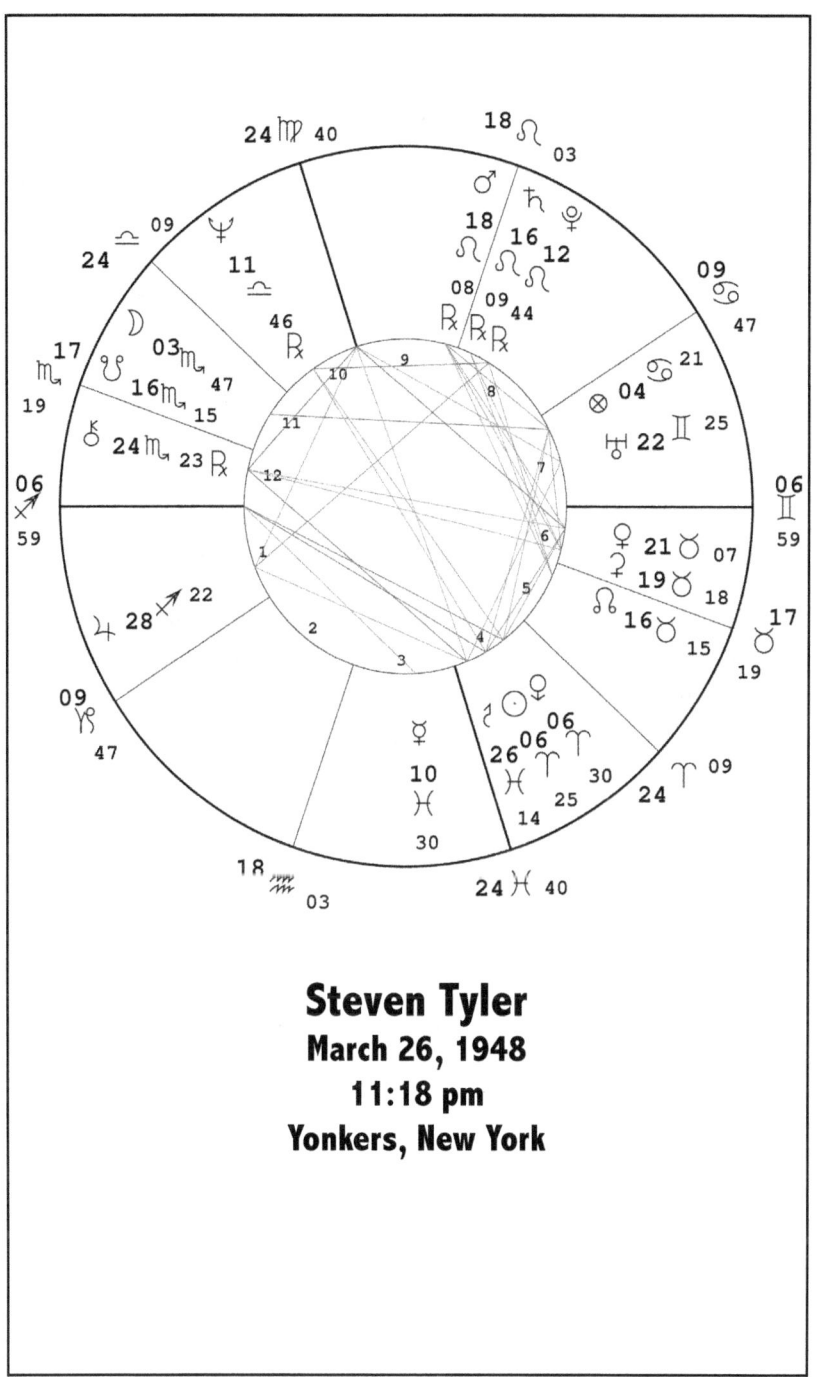

that it is healing for Steven to work in a group setting at this time, even though difficult with the opposition. This is challenging and he will grow. This is especially true with Hidalgo at 26 Pisces in the fourth house sextile Ceres. His foundational values of which Hidalgo plays a large part are healing with his work. His work is music and he is in a band (a small group) and plays for many people in every country (a large group of fans). This will help him overcome the ADD/ADHD. As I said before, sports and music are a great help in coping with ADD/ADHD.

His music was a large help to him. Hidalgo inconjunct or quincunx Mars by a very wide orb in Leo is also telling about his drive to be a showman, as well as of the ADD/ADHD. Hidalgo is opposite the Virgo cusp of the tenth house or Midheaven and square Jupiter in his first house, so the Hidalgo effect is expanded to him personally. Since Jupiter is in Sagittarius, natural sign of the ninth house, this indicates that ninth house activities of higher consciousness, philosophy and religion are also suggested. This is where Hidalgo ties in with his higher aspirations.

Hidalgo is sextile Venus in Taurus in the sixth house of health and work, so this helps him deal with the ADD/ADHD.

All the placements listed above support the ADD/ADHD and many of them, fortunately for Steven, also help him deal with it.

The true tell is Hidalgo square Uranus in the seventh house in Gemini. Hidalgo square Uranus is a very strong indication of ADD/ADHD, and since it is in Gemini, this placement relates to his mental activity. There is a lot of mental chaos here. His ability to concentrate is very erratic.

Hidalgo is trine Chiron in the twelfth house. Chiron is a place that needs healing, and in the twelfth house, suggests deeply buried reasons. Since Chiron is in Scorpio, it has to do with psychological factors and matters of the eighth house, such as endings and karma. This trine will help him deal with the ADD/ADHD, but Mars rules Scorpio, as well as Pluto, so his stellium of three planets all retrograde in Leo are involved. In fact, the Chiron placement in the twelfth house of hidden matters ruled by Mars and Pluto, is of itself, alone, a strong indication of the ADD/ADHD.

Although Chiron is opposite Venus in the house of health,

suggesting possible problems with health that need healing, Venus can help Steven deal with his ADD/ADHD, especially through his music. He is in a good position to manage well with his ADD/ADHD through his involvement in the arts and music.

Hidalgo is at the Jupiter/Uranus midpoint. This is also a strong indication of ADD/ADHD. With Jupiter in Sagittarius, higher consciousness and religion may play a part, and with Jupiter in the first house, it is personal. Uranus is in Gemini, so his erratic mind is involved. Hidalgo is in the fourth house of his foundation, so karmically, Steven's ADD/ADHD is foundational based on higher consciousness, and is an indicator of erratic and chaotic mental activity.

With Mercury in Pisces in his third house, Steven probably daydreamed his way through school, and with ADD/ADHD, school was probably not very much fun for him. However, Mercury in Pisces in the third house is also wonderful for imagination, intuition and the like, so it indicates his song writing ability.

Although Hidalgo is quincunx Mars in the ninth house by a wide orb, Mars is also part of a stellium in Leo, so Steven's quest for fame is influenced by Hidalgo. He wants to perform, and with the Hidalgo influence, he can hide somewhat behind the ADD/ADHD while he can still perform on stage.

Hidalgo is opposite the Midheaven. Steven was famous, as shown by his retrograde planets in Leo. Now, in one way, he wants to hide that for which he is famous, while still repeating the fame factor.

There is a T-square with Uranus in Gemini in the seventh house, the Midheaven and Jupiter in Sagittarius in the first house. This is very telling. Here we have square energy between Uranus in Gemini or the chaotic mind, and Jupiter in Sagittarius. This is an expansion of this chaos, with Sagittarius suggesting matters of higher consciousness. These placements are not retrograde. They are in the here and now, suggesting a repetition of the past, especially in the light of Hidalgo and his other planets that are retrograde.

Chiron retrograde is quincunx Uranus in Gemini. This is also very telling and very interesting. Uranus in Gemini is erratic thought patterns, and is quincunx a place in need of healing, the subconscious mind. Here is another indication of ADD/ADHD. Chiron in Scorpio suggests past activities of a psychological nature, investigation and clandestine matters from which the ADD/ADHD may stem.

There is a trine with the Sun in Aries in the fourth house, Pluto retrograde in Leo is in the eighth house. This is very telling with regard to his career. The trine energy gives an easy flow between Pluto in Leo, his showman comfort zone, his extreme energy and drive iwth the Sun in Aries. All of this energy is great for his creative Neputne in his tenth house.

Mercury in Pisces in the third house, again, shows that his song writing is prominent. His finger of fate points to who he is today, and despite his defense mechanism, he communicates through his art. Pisces is ruled by the retrograde Neptune in the tenth house, so he intuitively created and communicated. However, Neptune retrograde also indicates someone who has worked for the underdog in the past, perhaps getting into trouble. This also supports the ADD/ADHD.

An Interesting Midpoint

Another interesting thing about the Saturn retrograde in Leo is the midpoint of Uranus and Neptune. Steven's obstacles and heavy karma are influenced by Neptune retrograde in the tenth house, and Uranus in Gemini. That the chaos of his mind causes obstacles is apparent with this midpoint, as well, and this is another strong indication of ADD/ADHD.

Since Pluto is in the eighth house, this again supports power struggles and suggests a reformer of the past using psychological or even clandestine measures, probably concerning government, in a very public way (the Leo), and who now may be trying to be public again, while at the same time using his defense mechanism of ADD/ADHD.

MICHAEL PHELPS

Michael Phelps was born June 30, 1985 in Baltimore, MD. I do not have a verifiable birth time, so I've used 12:00 noon. This will work for the purpose of identifying ADD/ADHD. He is an

Olympic athlete. (See his chart on page 71.) As I have found with others with ADD or ADHD, athletics helps in concentration. It is a wonderful aid in coping with ADD/ADHD.,In Michael's case, he also had a great deal of talent. Athletics are one area in which the ADD/ADHD person can excel. With regard to his fame, the first thing I notice in his chart is that his Sun and Mars are in Cancer which is an indication of drive and strength in water. Ceres which is the nurturer is conjunct his Sun—strength and drive—so swimming is almost like being home. It is therapeutic for him. His South Node is in Scorpio, another water sign. It is conjunct Saturn retrograde by a slightly wide orb, so he swam before. In fact, since Saturn is retrograde, he is in his comfort zone when swimming. He will definitely shine with his Sun in a water sign. His Mars in Cancer is trine his South Node in Scorpio so his energy and strength are amazing.

Ceres is conjunct Michael's Sun and the water is his nurturer. He is home here.

Michael's Hidalgo is 18 Sagittarius, conjunct his retrograde Uranus at 15 degrees Sagittarius. The sign of Sagittarius suggests higher consciousness linked with Hidalgo, and with Uranus, comes chaos. Uranus is retrograde, and suggests a link to past conditions with higher consciousness and what could be one root cause of ADD/ADHD. He was a rebel in the past and his rebelliousness was based on higher consciousness matters. Hidalgo conjunct Uranus retrograde is a strong indicator of possible ADD/ADHD.

Saturn is retrograde and conjunct the South Node in Scorpio by a slightly wide orb, so Michael is carrying a lot of heavy karma. Saturn retrograde, alone, would suggest heavy obstacles and in Scorpio it appears as though the clandestine activity or activities of an eighth house nature come into play. Combine this with his Uranus retrograde rebelliousness from a past life, and you can see another strong indication of the ADD/ADHD, especially with Uranus conjunct Hidalgo. Here is a person with past life power struggles, a reformer and rebel, all linked to the martyr Hidalgo.

He has a yod aspect (also called "finger of fate") with Hidalgo, Uranus, the North Node and Mars. This is also very telling. The North Node and Mars point toward Hidalgo and Uranus. The North Node is in Taurus. Regardless of the houses, the Yod has these significant points:

1. Mars in Cancer (ruler of the fourth house or foundation and the end of matters). This suggests a martyr (the Hidalgo part of the Yod) for foundational beliefs.

2. The North Node, although karmic to me, is also what you are doing in this lifetime, and Mars represents drive and energy. Michael's North Node and his Mars (in sextile to each other), point by quincunx aspects toward the conjunction of Uranus and Hidalgo in Sagittarius. The North Node represents what he wants to do now, while Mars represents the drive and energy,. They both point by yod aspects toward the conjunction of Uranus retrograde and Hidalgo in Sagittarius. A yod configuration such as this has been termed by some a "finger of fate." Whatever Michael did before (with his higher consciousness of a rebel and reformer) to create a need for the ADD/ADHD, he wants to do it again. Swimming is his way to communicate with the world. This is very interesting in his chart. The Uranus retrograde conjunct Hidalgo is the history of the rebel and of chaos repeating itself, since the North Node (this lifetime); and Mars (his drive), both point to the placement.

    As you can see from the Yod, you do not necessarily have to consider the planets in their houses in order to see their relationship when it comes to ADD/ADHD.

    Both Pluto and the South Node are in Scorpio. Pluto also rules Scorpio, and Pluto is retrograde. Michael tried to reorganize and reform, perhaps because he had extreme power struggles in past live(s). There is an element of psychology, secrets, and eighth house types of matters since Scorpio rules the eighth house. This is a clue as to where he may have gotten into trouble in the past. However, I do feel that the type of martyr that seems to have ADD/ADHD is the type who works *for* humanity, even if clandestine or with Scorpio sting, as is demonstrated with his Uranus and Hidalgo in Sagittarius. The North Node is quincunx Hidalgo, so he must work very hard now to overcome the ADD/ADHD.

    Mars is also quincunx Hidalgo, and again is in Cancer,

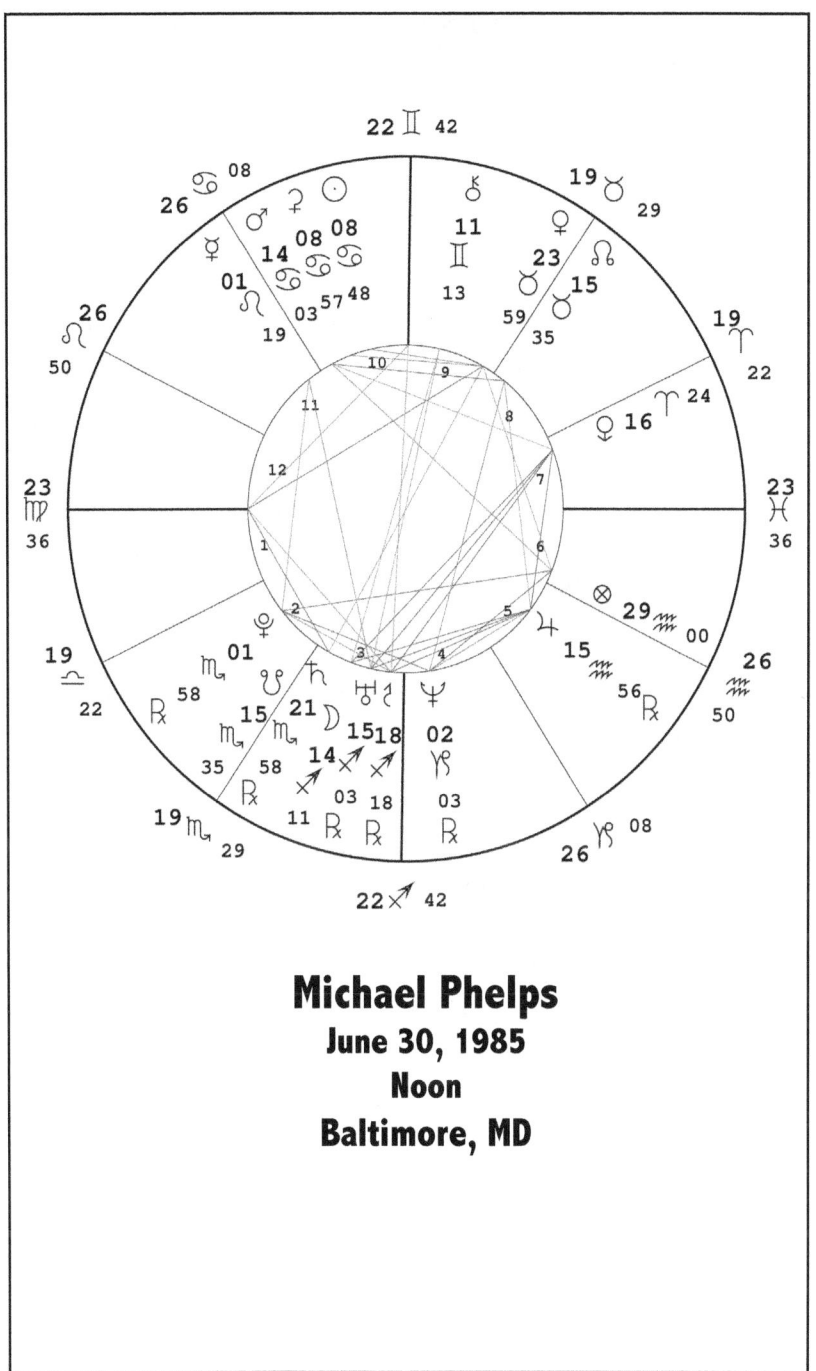

Michael Phelps
June 30, 1985
Noon
Baltimore, MD

thus his foundational beliefs or his core are greatly influenced by the manifestations of Hidalgo. Also, since Mars is in Cancer, he has a push and pull with expression—if he has feelings about something, it will be hard for him to express. This goes a long way with ADD/ADHD. He feels strongly and has gotten into trouble in a past life or lives, so why would he express his feelings now?

On the other hand, the Mars in Cancer suggests the strong swimmer and obviously sports will help him cope with the ADD/ADHD. He has a desire to nurture but also protect, including protecting himself with his ADD/ADHD defense mechanisms.

Chiron (by a wide orb) is opposite Hidalgo and is in Gemini (or mental activity) opposing the ramifications of Hidalgo, being Chiron opposite Uranus and within orb. Here is another indication of ADD/ADHD. Chiron is a place for healing, Uranus is the chaos that needs to be healed, and since Uranus is in Sagittarius, his higher ideals have caused this need for healing.

Just these few placements with Hidalgo show how Michael may have ADD or ADHD. This is evident even without a true birth time. You can see it is planetary relationships that are far more influential than the house within which they sit that suggest ADD/ADHD. Although there are a couple of wide orbs used in my delineation, I feel the aspects reinforce the very strong placement of Hidalgo conjunct Uranus retrograde in Sagittarius.

Also Michael's Neptune Retrograde is opposite his Sun by a slightly wide orb, although retrograding back toward Sun, so here we have a past life of perhaps taking on problems of those around him, especially by intuitive empathy, and this may be a cause of difficulty for him now.

Pluto, currently retrograde in Scorpio, is square his natal Mercury, suggesting an effect on his mental activity, as well. His past reformer actions may now affect his mind and since Pluto is in Scorpio, eighth house activities are included in the mix. Mercury is in Leo, and he will be able to communicate when he is in the spotlight. Uranus, which plays such a part in his ADD/ADHD placements with Hidalgo, is quincunx Mars in the water sign of Cancer. His drive to swim is really helping Michael cope with his ADD/ADHD. His Sun is trine Pluto and that shows his personal strength, the strength of a past life reformer.

Michael's most important Yod for strength of purpose is Hidalgo/Uranus retrograde and Jupiter retrograde pointing toward Mars. Here again we have Uranus retrograde in Sagittarius bringing in chaos, the rebel and Sagittarius higher consciousness, the Hidalgo martyr,. Also, Jupiter retrograde is expanding the Uranus/Hidalgo influence and is pointing toward Mars in Cancer, which is foundational or core to Michael. Jupiter is in Aquarius and Michael could also benefit from new technology or contribute to new technology (perhaps new swim wear for efficiency). Jupiter is a benevolent planet and although expansive in light of the ADD/ADHD, it also helps open doors he has earned in past live(s).

HOWIE MANDEL

Howie Mandel was born November 29, 1955, 10:00 A.M. in Toronto, Ontario, Canada. He is a stand up comedian, actor, game show host, and judge on *America's Got Talent*. See his chart on page 75.

Howie is very successful, despite ADD/ADHD. At a cursory glance, he has Saturn in his tenth house which is karmic, so what he does to create his fame and notoriety will come from past conditions. He will also have to work very hard and fight obstacles along the way. His Pluto, co-ruler of Scorpio, is in Leo in the eighth house, in an out-of-sign conjunction to Jupiter in the beginning of Virgo. Leo, here, is the actor or showman and Pluto suggests power, struggle and reform.

Since the eighth house suggests endings, it may also suggest karma. He now wants to reform and to have power through his showmanship. He may have tried to reform the world with the use of his showmanship abilities in a past life, somewhat like acting with a message or purpose. This idea stems from Pluto being in the eighth house which is about death, rebirth and psychology as well as karma. His Sun, Mercury and North Node are in the eleventh house of groups, but in Sagittarius, which suggests that higher ideals and reform are a key to making money in his profession (using derivative houses). Of course, actors are the group he has chosen in which to shine. Also, the eleventh is the house of friends, and they will share his ideals.

The astrological placements contributing to ADD/ADHD are:

Eleventh House karmic Hidalgo is 8 Sagittarius conjunct his Mercury at 3 Sagittarius and Sun at 6 Sagittarius. The North Node is also in the eleventh house at 17 Sagittarius, too wide for conjunction to the other three, but still, it contributes to the strength in this house. Sagittarius represents a person with high ideals and a strong higher consciousness. With the conjunction to Hidalgo in the eleventh house, these placements also suggest a person associated with a group that acted for the good of society, but then got into trouble in the process.

Again, Hidalgo remains in Sagittarius a long time, but people often reincarnate with generational conditions affecting who they are now. With such a close conjunction to the Sun (2 degrees), Hidalgo is a very strong personal influence. It represents how and/or where he will shine and as such, affects his person completely. This connection to a luminary is one of the strongest indicators of potential ADD/ADHD.

More importantly, Hidalgo is part of a T-square with the Moon in Gemini at 5 degrees, and since Gemini is the mind, this affects Howie's ability to be attentive. There is a great deal of fluctuation in his thought processes (fluctuation being the Moon influence) and he is very emotional about his condition. Jupiter is also part of the T-Square. Jupiter is expansion, so is expanding his ADD/ADHD. Jupiter is at 0 degrees Virgo in the eighth house which is conjunct the Pluto in Leo, as previously mentioned.

Mars is at 0 degrees Scorpio is in the ninth house of, among other things, higher consciousness, religion and philosophy. Mars is the co-ruler of Scorpio. In the ninth house, it appears that his strength in eighth house matters has the addition of a higher consciousness. Since I view the eighth house as karmic, it appears that his activities may have been clandestine, with Mars in Scorpio, while his persona was in the public eye. This could be an actor, reporter, or with the eighth house relating to taxes, someone with control in the government or someone who has great psychological or psychic influence. Since the Sun and Mercury are in Sagittarius they bring in ninth house matters as

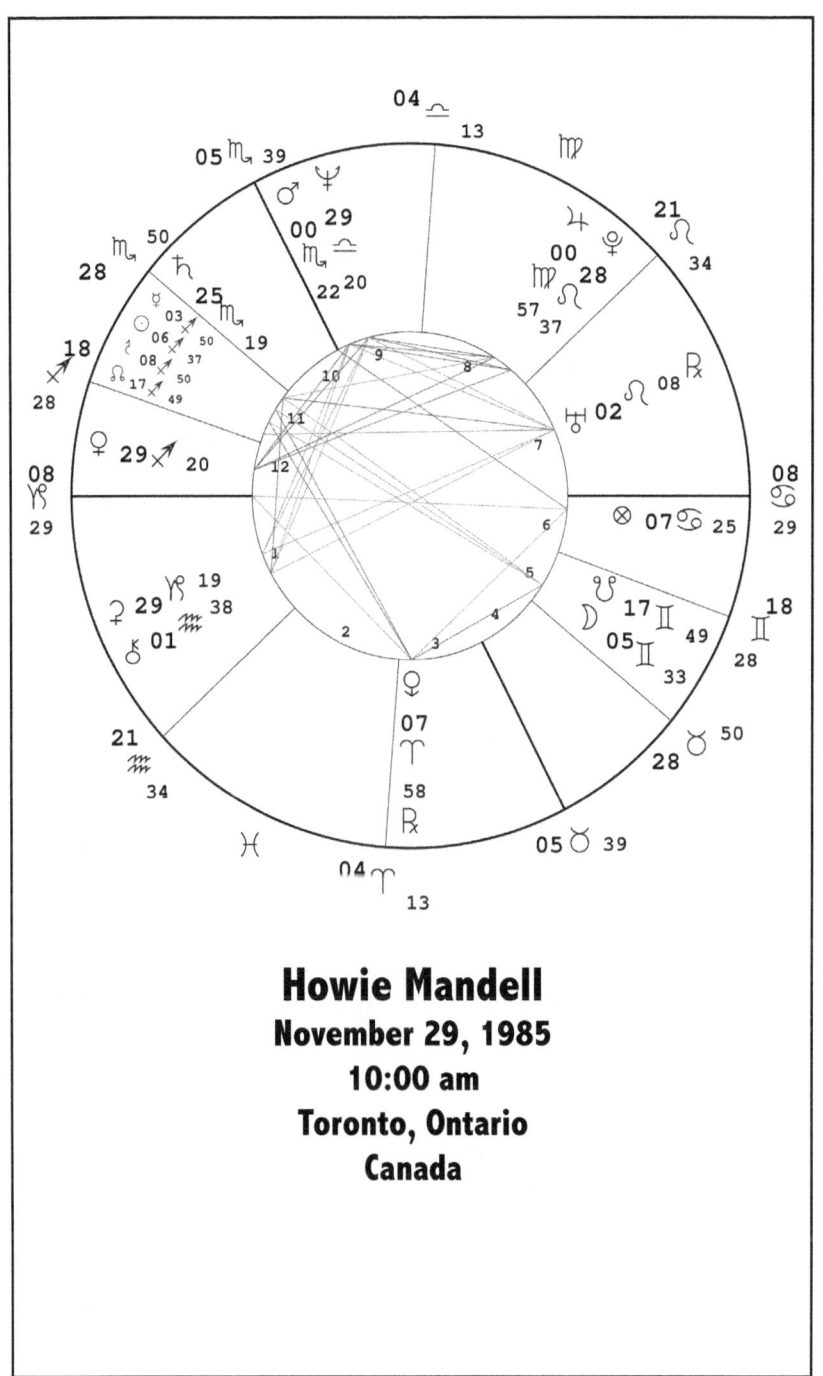

Howie Mandell
November 29, 1985
10:00 am
Toronto, Ontario
Canada

well. This is the true indication of Hidalgo's influence as part of this T-Square. As you can see there is a strong connection with higher consciousness, past clandestine activities with a ninth house focus, a reformer or a power struggle, all of which are tied to Hidalgo—the catalyst suggesting the ADD/ADHD.

There is also a T-square with Uranus retrograde in Leo, Mars in Scorpio in the ninth house, Neptune at 29 degrees Libra in the ninth house, the Midheaven in Scorpio and Chiron in the first house. Wow—here is the ADD/ADHD!

Then, we have the chaos of Uranus which is retrograde in Leo, so here Howie is repeating the showmanship, right along with his drive from Mars in Scorpio, natural ruler of the eighth house of karma, clandestine matters, and psychology. Neptune is insight, but also confusion, and there is a personal need for healing with Chiron in the first house. Neptune is in Libra, so he is seeking a balance—but since it is in the ninth house, he may still take on the problems of the world. This is such a tough T-square! I think it took him a long time to cope with his ADD/ADHD.

There is a three planet stellium with Neptune at 29 Libra conjunct Mars at the 0 degree of Scorpio, and the Midheaven at 5 degrees Scorpio. Neptune is in Libra which is ruled by Venus at 29 Sagittarius in the twelfth house. I consider this to be quite important, because Sagittarius, representing higher consciousness, in the twelfth house of the subconscious at 29 degrees, suggests a lack of control. This could create conditions not brought to the surface, but instead, manifesting themselves on a much deeper level. Since benevolent Venus is involved, Howie is aided in his ability to act and to be a comedian. Comic ability gives him a profession within which he may change and move quickly from one thing to the other—so, this is very good for ADD/ADHD. He has a subconscious coping mechanism. Neptune in the ninth house gives him worldwide notoriety.

He has a Rosetta with Chiron (a place needing healing) in his first house in Aquarius. If he was not a comedian, he may well have been at the forefront of technology in a rapidly changing world that would have helped him to cope. He would quickly adapt to changing technology. The Rosetta also includes the

Moon in Gemini in the fifth house, Jupiter at 0 degrees in Virgo in the eighth house, Mars at 0 Scorpio in the ninth house and on the cusp of the 10th house, and Neptune at 29 Libra in the ninth house—very telling.

A Rosetta configuration consists of planets that have friends (trines), but at the same time, also enemies (squares), and each and every planet in the configuration has both friends and enemies. In this case, for example, the Mercury and Chiron are sextile but Chiron is square Mars and Neptune. Also Moon is trine Chiron, but also square both Jupiter and (widely) Pluto.

Often a Rosetta configuration indicates going around and around in circles, sometimes not accomplishing anything. It is almost ADD/ADHD in nature. There is a great deal of fluctuation or change with the Moon in Gemini, but Moon is in the fifth house of creativity, art and children, so even though it may contribute to his ADD/ADHD, it also shows Howie Mandel's very quick, changeable mind and his ability to be very quick on his feet as a comedian. What a coping mechanism! Although many people have Rosettas, and most do not necessarily have ADD/ADHD, because of his Hidalgo conjunct Mercury, and that, along with his Sun and other placements discussed, Howie's ADD/ADHD is somewhat apparent.

The Moon, Chiron, Eris and Ceres are below the horizon, with the remainder of the planets above the horizon, so he cannot help but be in the public eye. Pluto in Leo in the eighth house suggests a showman who has power struggles, works to reform and has a lot of opportunity to do so, since Pluto is conjunct Jupiter. Again, Pluto is co-ruler (with Mars) of Scorpio, so this carries into his tenth house of profession.

Hidalgo is also opposite the Moon in Gemini. ADD/ADHD affects his mental ability and may cause many changes in creativity, as well. The Sun and Moon have a push and pull with his consciousness and his higher consciousness, since they are in Sagittarius (ruler of ninth house higher consciousness) and Gemini (ruler of third house of conscious mind). So...back and forth, back and forth.

The South Node is in the fifth house of creativity which

reinforces the eighth house Pluto. He has been creative in prior lives, and since his karmic South Node is in Gemini, this relates to his mind and its function. It also suggests that his comfort zone is mental since it opposes his Sagittarius planets. He must find a balance of quick and erratic mental ability with his higher consciousness.

I think he has done so—his profession gives him the perfect outlet to just let his mind go. This opposition of communication with the South Node in Gemini opposite his Hidalgo in Sagittarius in the eleventh house of groups is another strong indication of past life conditions being affected by higher consciousness and being a member of a group much like the man Hidalgo, perhaps a martyr. It appears that the Hidalgo position within the T-Square with the South Node in Gemini and conjunct is Sun is very influential on Howie's life and career.

Another factor to consider is that Sagittarius is ruled by Jupiter, which sits in Howie's eighth house, thus his Hidalgo, Sun, Mercury and the North Node are ruled by the planet in his eighth house of psychological matters and karma.

Neptune in the ninth house at 29 degrees Libra is in sextile to the exact degree of Venus in the twelfth house of hidden conditions and subconcious. There is help with benevolent Venus and his subconscious coming into play with his higher consciousness. He probably has dreams or flashes of inspiration from his subconsious. Sagittarius is the natural ruler of the ninth house, so his subconscious or past life connects within a higher consciousness, humane issues, and at the same time, also support ADD/ADHD. Venus is benevolent and may help ease the pressure a bit.

I would have thought Saturn might have been a bit more prominent in his ADD/ADHD placements. Since it squares Pluto in the Eighth House, it also can be taken to increase the Pluto influence on his ADD/ADHD. Hidalgo is so very strong in Howie's chart, such that Saturn's usual influence is felt, but does not need to be as strong. However, Saturn square Pluto in the eighth house can mean that, again, we have clandestine Scorpio mixed with psychological matters. This suggests power struggle and reformation, so there is some indication in his chart of his

ADD/ADHD supported here, as well.

When looking at the two newly named planets in this chart, the first thing that pops out is that Ceres is at the critical 29th degree in the first house. The 29th degree suggests that you do not have control, and with Ceres here, he will feel a need for nurturing—to help cope. Ceres is very closely square the conjunction of Neptune at 29 Libra and Mars at 0 Scorpio in the ninth house. In Neptune Ceres, we have the nurturer or the idealist looking for equity and balance, and Mars the warrior, both in the ninth house of higher consciousness, and also of the priest or professor. You see the idealist with a lot of intuition coming out in him, and his need to take care of himself in order to cope with this. None of these planets are retrograde, but they do express Howie Mandel now, and he seems to be repeating past patterns.

Ceres is also conjunct Chiron, so this nurturing is a way to heal. Ceres is sextile his Saturn at 25 degrees Scorpio in his tenth house, so his public personal also helps him feel good about himself.

Eris is 7 degrees Aries, retrograde in the third house. Howie was probably attempting to reform or transform via speaking out, and is in his comfort zone speaking again.

Howie Mandel's placements suggest someone who is definitely in the public eye now because of being also very much in public at a prior time when he may have used his position—probably acting or speaking out, but also perhaps working in a clandestine manner—to promote a humane cause. This is solely because of relationships between the planets that are retrograde and Hidalgo—along with rulership and house influence. He is a poster boy for ADD/ADHD and of how one can learn to cope with it and then use it for his own well-being, as well as for the public good.

Summary

As you can see from the charts analyzed, you must look at a lot of natal charts in order to see the patterns of ADD/ADHD. After looking for quite some time, it becomes apparent. I suggest you start with the karmic Hidalgo placement and its relationship to other planets and go from there.

BIBLIOGRAPHY

Articles

Living and Coping With ADHD by Gayle L. Zieman, Ph.D. in *The Challenge of Hidalgo* by Zane B. Stein, circa 1981
Lecture notes of Lynn Koiner on both Eris and Ceres
Lecture notes of Lynn Koiner on the Lobes of the Brain
Father Miguel Hidalgo and the Mexican Revolution by Jeffrey Robenault, Texasescapes.com
Mexican Independence, Sons of Dewitt Colony Texas www.tamu.edu/faculty/ccbn/dewittmexicanrev.htm
Miquel Hidalgo y Costilla Wikipedia

Books

Astrology at a Glance, Barbara Harkins & Gayle Lakin-Geffner, Harlak Press 1986

A-Z Horoscope Maker, Llewellyn George, Llewellyn Publications, 1978 Edition

Rulership Book, Rex E. Bills, American Federation of Astrologers 1989 Edition

Yod, Miss Dee, American Federation of Astrologers, 1989 Edition

The Yod Book, Karen Hamaker-Zondag, Samuel Weiser, Inc.,

Lunar Nodes Mohan Koparkar, Ph.D., Mohan Enterprises

Twelve Faces of Saturn, Bil Tierney, Llewellyn Publications, 1997

Yankee Doodle Discord, Thomas Canfield, ACS Publications, 2010.

Ceres in Signs, Houses, Aspects, Simonne Murphy, ACS Publications, 2013.

A Brief History of Mexico, Lynn V. Foster, Checkmark Books 4th Ed. 2009

Super Parenting for ADD, by Peter S. Jensen, M.D., published by Ballantine Books - New York 2010 Trade Paperback Edition.

ADHD What Every Parent Needs to Know, 2nd Edition by Michael I. Reiff, M.D., FAAP Editor in Chief

HIDALGO TABLES

1950 - 2100

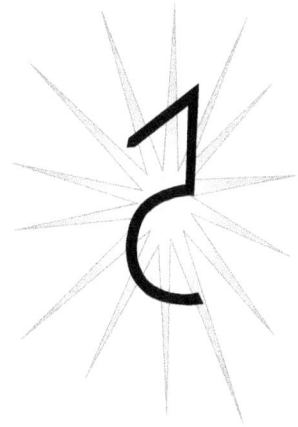

For your convenience in reading this book and in relating Hidalgo to your own life, we are providing an ephemeris of Hidalgo, so that you can look up the sign and degree of where your own is, and also that of others—providing you were born from 1950 forward. If you were born earlier, please see on page 101 how you can order charts or calculations from Astro Computing Services for any year, past, present or future, that include Hidalgo.

Col 1	Col 2	Col 3	Col 4
1950	9/27 10 ♏ 00	6/24 2 ♐ 00R	3/20 7 ♑ 00
1/ 1 17 ♎ 01	10/17 12 ♏ 01	7/14 0 ♐ 01R	4/ 9 8 ♑ 00
1/21 19 ♎ 00	11/ 6 15 ♏ 01	8/ 3 29 ♏ 01R	4/29 7 ♑ 01R
2/10 18 ♎ 00R	11/26 18 ♏ 00	8/23 29 ♏ 01	5/19 6 ♑ 00R
3/ 2 15 ♎ 01R	12/16 20 ♏ 01	9/12 0 ♐ 01	6/ 8 4 ♑ 00R
3/22 11 ♎ 01R	**1953**	10/ 2 2 ♐ 00	6/28 1 ♑ 00R
4/11 7 ♎ 00R	1/ 5 22 ♏ 01	10/22 4 ♐ 00	7/18 28 ♐ 01R
5/ 1 3 ♎ 01R	1/25 24 ♏ 01	11/11 6 ♐ 00	8/ 7 26 ♐ 01R
5/21 2 ♎ 00R	2/14 25 ♏ 00	12/ 1 9 ♐ 00	8/27 25 ♐ 01R
6/10 2 ♎ 00	3/ 6 25 ♏ 00R	12/21 11 ♐ 01	9/16 25 ♐ 01
6/30 3 ♎ 00	3/26 24 ♏ 01R	**1956**	10/ 6 26 ♐ 01
7/20 5 ♎ 01	4/15 22 ♏ 01R	1/10 14 ♐ 00	10/26 28 ♐ 00
8/ 9 8 ♎ 01	5/ 5 20 ♏ 01R	1/30 16 ♐ 00	11/15 0 ♑ 01
8/29 12 ♎ 00	5/25 18 ♏ 00R	2/19 17 ♐ 01	12/ 5 3 ♑ 01
9/18 16 ♎ 00	6/14 16 ♏ 00R	3/10 18 ♐ 01	12/25 7 ♑ 00
10/ 8 20 ♎ 00	7/ 4 14 ♏ 01R	3/30 18 ♐ 01R	**1959**
10/28 24 ♎ 00	7/24 14 ♏ 00R	4/19 17 ♐ 01R	1/14 10 ♑ 00
11/17 28 ♎ 00	8/13 14 ♏ 01	5/ 9 15 ♐ 01R	2/ 3 13 ♑ 01
12/ 7 1 ♏ 01	9/ 2 15 ♏ 01	5/29 13 ♐ 01R	2/23 16 ♑ 01
12/27 4 ♏ 00	9/22 17 ♏ 00	6/18 11 ♐ 00R	3/15 19 ♑ 00
1951	10/12 19 ♏ 01	7/ 8 9 ♐ 00R	4/ 4 20 ♑ 01
1/16 6 ♏ 00	11/ 1 21 ♏ 01	7/28 7 ♐ 01R	4/24 21 ♑ 00
2/ 5 6 ♏ 01	11/21 24 ♏ 01	8/17 7 ♐ 00R	5/14 21 ♑ 00R
2/25 6 ♏ 00R	12/11 27 ♏ 00	9/ 6 7 ♐ 01	6/ 3 19 ♑ 01R
3/17 4 ♏ 01R	12/31 29 ♏ 00	9/26 8 ♐ 01	6/23 17 ♑ 00R
4/ 6 2 ♏ 00R	**1954**	10/16 10 ♐ 01	7/13 14 ♑ 00R
4/26 29 ♎ 00R	1/20 1 ♐ 00	11/ 5 12 ♐ 01	8/ 2 11 ♑ 00R
5/16 26 ♎ 00R	2/ 9 2 ♐ 01	11/25 15 ♐ 00	8/22 8 ♑ 01R
6/ 5 24 ♎ 00R	3/ 1 3 ♐ 00	12/15 18 ♐ 00	9/11 7 ♑ 01R
6/25 23 ♎ 00R	3/21 2 ♐ 01R	**1957**	10/ 1 8 ♑ 00
7/15 23 ♎ 01	4/10 1 ♐ 01R	1/ 4 20 ♐ 01	10/21 9 ♑ 00
8/ 4 24 ♎ 01	4/30 29 ♏ 01R	1/24 23 ♐ 00	11/10 11 ♑ 01
8/24 26 ♎ 01	5/20 27 ♏ 01R	2/13 25 ♐ 00	11/30 14 ♑ 01
9/13 29 ♎ 00	6/ 9 25 ♏ 00R	3/ 5 26 ♐ 01	12/20 18 ♑ 00
10/ 3 1 ♏ 01	6/29 23 ♏ 01R	3/25 27 ♐ 00	**1960**
10/23 5 ♏ 00	7/19 22 ♏ 01R	4/14 27 ♐ 00R	1/ 9 21 ♑ 01
11/12 8 ♏ 00	8/ 8 22 ♏ 00	5/ 4 26 ♐ 00R	1/29 25 ♑ 01
12/ 2 11 ♏ 00	8/28 22 ♏ 01	5/24 24 ♐ 00R	2/18 29 ♑ 01
12/22 13 ♏ 01	9/17 23 ♏ 01	6/13 21 ♐ 01R	3/ 9 3 ♒ 00
1952	10/ 7 25 ♏ 01	7/ 3 19 ♐ 00R	3/29 6 ♒ 00
1/11 15 ♏ 01	10/27 27 ♏ 01	7/23 17 ♐ 00R	4/18 8 ♒ 01
1/31 16 ♏ 01	11/16 0 ♐ 00	8/12 16 ♐ 00R	5/ 8 9 ♒ 01
2/20 17 ♏ 00R	12/ 6 3 ♐ 00	9/ 1 15 ♐ 01	5/28 9 ♒ 01R
3/11 16 ♏ 01R	12/26 5 ♐ 00	9/21 16 ♐ 00	6/17 8 ♒ 01R
3/31 15 ♏ 00R	**1955**	10/11 17 ♐ 01	7/ 7 5 ♒ 01R
4/20 12 ♏ 01R	1/15 7 ♐ 01	10/31 19 ♐ 01	7/27 2 ♒ 00R
5/10 10 ♏ 00R	2/ 4 9 ♐ 00	11/20 22 ♐ 00	8/16 28 ♑ 01R
5/30 7 ♏ 01R	2/24 10 ♐ 00	12/10 25 ♐ 00	9/ 5 26 ♑ 00R
6/19 6 ♏ 00R	3/16 10 ♐ 01R	12/30 28 ♐ 00	9/25 24 ♑ 01R
7/ 9 5 ♏ 00R	4/ 5 10 ♐ 00R	**1958**	10/15 25 ♑ 00
7/29 5 ♏ 01	4/25 8 ♐ 01R	1/19 1 ♑ 00	11/ 4 26 ♑ 01
8/18 6 ♏ 00	5/15 6 ♐ 01R	2/ 8 3 ♑ 01	11/24 29 ♑ 00
9/ 7 8 ♏ 00	6/ 4 4 ♐ 00R	2/28 5 ♑ 01	12/14 2 ♒ 01

1961	9/30 23 ♍ 00	6/26 6 ♏ 00R	3/22 10 ♐ 01R
1/ 3 7 ♒ 00	10/20 0 ♎ 01	7/16 5 ♏ 01R	4/11 9 ♐ 01R
1/23 11 ♒ 01	11/ 9 7 ♎ 00	8/ 5 5 ♏ 01	5/ 1 8 ♐ 00R
2/12 16 ♒ 01	11/29 12 ♎ 00	8/25 7 ♏ 00	5/21 6 ♐ 00R
3/ 4 21 ♒ 01	12/19 16 ♎ 00	9/14 8 ♏ 01	6/10 3 ♐ 01R
3/24 26 ♒ 00	**1964**	10/ 4 11 ♏ 00	6/30 1 ♐ 01R
4/13 0 ♓ 01	1/ 8 18 ♎ 01	10/24 13 ♏ 01	7/20 0 ♐ 00R
5/ 3 4 ♓ 00	1/28 19 ♎ 01R	11/13 16 ♏ 01	8/ 9 29 ♏ 01R
5/23 7 ♓ 00	2/17 18 ♎ 00R	12/ 3 19 ♏ 00	8/29 0 ♐ 00
6/12 8 ♓ 01	3/ 8 15 ♎ 00R	12/23 21 ♏ 01	9/18 1 ♐ 00
7/ 2 8 ♓ 01R	3/28 10 ♎ 01R	**1967**	10/ 8 2 ♐ 01
7/22 7 ♓ 00R	4/17 6 ♎ 01R	1/12 23 ♏ 01	10/28 4 ♐ 01
8/11 3 ♓ 01R	5/ 7 4 ♎ 00R	2/ 1 25 ♏ 00	11/17 7 ♐ 00
8/31 29 ♒ 00R	5/27 2 ♎ 01R	2/21 25 ♏ 01	12/ 7 9 ♐ 01
9/20 25 ♒ 00R	6/16 3 ♎ 00	3/13 25 ♏ 00R	12/27 12 ♐ 00
10/10 22 ♒ 00R	7/ 6 4 ♎ 01	4/ 2 24 ♏ 00R	**1970**
10/30 21 ♒ 01	7/26 7 ♎ 00	4/22 22 ♏ 00R	1/16 14 ♐ 01
11/19 23 ♒ 00	8/15 10 ♎ 00	5/12 20 ♏ 00R	2/ 5 16 ♐ 01
12/ 9 26 ♒ 00	9/ 4 14 ♎ 00	6/ 1 17 ♏ 01R	2/25 18 ♐ 00
12/29 0 ♓ 00	9/24 18 ♎ 00	6/21 15 ♏ 01R	3/17 18 ♐ 01
1962	10/14 22 ♎ 00	7/11 14 ♏ 01R	4/ 6 18 ♐ 00R
1/18 5 ♓ 00	11/ 3 26 ♎ 00	7/31 14 ♏ 01	4/26 17 ♐ 00R
2/ 7 11 ♓ 00	11/23 29 ♎ 01	8/20 15 ♏ 00	5/16 15 ♐ 00R
2/27 17 ♓ 01	12/13 2 ♏ 01	9/ 9 16 ♏ 00	6/ 5 13 ♐ 00R
3/19 24 ♓ 00	**1965**	9/29 18 ♏ 00	6/25 10 ♐ 01R
4/ 8 1 ♈ 00	1/ 2 5 ♏ 00	10/19 20 ♏ 00	7/15 8 ♐ 01R
4/28 8 ♈ 00	1/22 6 ♏ 01	11/ 8 22 ♏ 01	8/ 4 7 ♐ 01R
5/18 15 ♈ 00	2/11 7 ♏ 00R	11/28 25 ♏ 00	8/24 7 ♐ 00
6/ 7 21 ♈ 01	3/ 3 6 ♏ 00R	12/18 27 ♏ 01	9/13 8 ♐ 00
6/27 28 ♈ 00	3/23 4 ♏ 00R	**1968**	10/ 3 9 ♐ 00
7/17 4 ♉ 00	4/12 1 ♏ 00R	1/ 7 0 ♐ 00	10/23 11 ♐ 00
8/ 6 9 ♉ 00	5/ 2 28 ♎ 00R	1/27 1 ♐ 01	11/12 13 ♐ 01
8/26 12 ♉ 01	5/22 25 ♎ 01R	2/16 2 ♐ 01	12/ 2 16 ♐ 00
9/15 14 ♉ 00	6/11 24 ♎ 00R	3/ 7 3 ♐ 00R	12/22 19 ♐ 00
10/ 5 13 ♉ 00R	7/ 1 23 ♎ 01R	3/27 2 ♐ 01R	**1971**
10/25 8 ♉ 00R	7/21 24 ♎ 00	4/16 1 ♐ 00R	1/11 21 ♐ 01
11/14 1 ♉ 01R	8/10 25 ♎ 01	5/ 6 29 ♏ 00R	1/31 23 ♐ 01
12/ 4 26 ♈ 01R	8/30 27 ♎ 01	5/26 27 ♏ 00R	2/20 25 ♐ 01
12/24 25 ♈ 01	9/19 0 ♏ 00	6/15 24 ♏ 01R	3/12 27 ♐ 00
1963	10/ 9 3 ♏ 00	7/ 5 23 ♏ 00R	4/ 1 27 ♐ 00R
1/13 29 ♈ 00	10/29 6 ♏ 00	7/25 22 ♏ 00R	4/21 26 ♐ 01R
2/ 2 6 ♉ 01	11/18 9 ♏ 00	8/14 22 ♏ 00	5/11 25 ♐ 01R
2/22 16 ♉ 01	12/ 8 12 ♏ 00	9/ 3 23 ♏ 00	5/31 23 ♐ 00R
3/14 29 ♉ 00	12/28 14 ♏ 00	9/23 24 ♏ 01	6/20 20 ♐ 01R
4/ 3 12 ♊ 01	**1966**	10/13 26 ♏ 00	7/10 18 ♐ 01R
4/23 26 ♊ 01	1/17 16 ♏ 00	11/ 2 28 ♏ 01	7/30 16 ♐ 01R
5/13 10 ♋ 00	2/ 6 17 ♏ 00	11/22 1 ♐ 00	8/19 15 ♐ 01R
6/ 2 23 ♋ 00	2/26 17 ♏ 00R	12/12 3 ♐ 01	9/ 8 15 ♐ 01
6/22 5 ♌ 01	3/18 16 ♏ 00R	**1969**	9/28 16 ♐ 01
7/12 16 ♌ 01	4/ 7 14 ♏ 00R	1/ 1 6 ♐ 00	10/18 18 ♐ 00
8/ 1 27 ♌ 00	4/27 12 ♏ 00R	1/21 8 ♐ 00	11/ 7 20 ♐ 01
8/21 6 ♍ 01	5/17 9 ♏ 01R	2/10 9 ♐ 01	11/27 23 ♐ 00
9/10 15 ♍ 00	6/ 6 7 ♏ 00R	3/ 2 10 ♐ 01	12/17 26 ♐ 00

Hidalgo Tables

1972	10/ 2 24 ♑ 00R	6/28 2 ♌ 00	3/24 14 ♏ 01R
1/ 6 29 ♐ 00	10/22 24 ♑ 01	7/18 14 ♌ 00	4/13 12 ♏ 01R
1/26 2 ♑ 00	11/11 26 ♑ 01	8/ 7 25 ♌ 00	5/ 3 10 ♏ 00R
2/15 4 ♑ 00	12/ 1 29 ♑ 01	8/27 5 ♍ 00	5/23 7 ♏ 01R
3/ 6 6 ♑ 00	12/21 3 ♒ 01	9/16 14 ♍ 00	6/12 5 ♏ 01R
3/26 7 ♑ 01	1975	10/ 6 22 ♍ 01	7/ 2 4 ♏ 01R
4/15 7 ♑ 01R	1/10 7 ♒ 01	10/26 29 ♍ 01	7/22 4 ♏ 01
5/ 5 7 ♑ 00R	1/30 12 ♒ 01	11/15 6 ♎ 00	8/11 5 ♏ 00
5/25 5 ♑ 01R	2/19 17 ♒ 00	12/ 5 11 ♎ 01	8/31 6 ♏ 01
6/14 3 ♑ 00R	3/11 22 ♒ 00	12/25 15 ♎ 00	9/20 8 ♏ 01
7/ 4 0 ♑ 00R	3/31 26 ♒ 01	1978	10/10 11 ♏ 00
7/24 27 ♐ 01R	4/20 0 ♓ 01	1/14 17 ♎ 00	10/30 14 ♏ 00
8/13 26 ♐ 00R	5/10 3 ♓ 01	2/ 3 17 ♎ 00R	11/19 16 ♏ 01
9/ 2 25 ♐ 00R	5/30 6 ♓ 00	2/23 14 ♎ 01R	12/ 9 19 ♏ 00
9/22 25 ♐ 01	6/19 7 ♓ 00	3/15 10 ♎ 01R	12/29 21 ♏ 01
10/12 27 ♐ 00	7/ 9 6 ♓ 00R	4/ 4 6 ♎ 00R	1981
11/ 1 29 ♐ 00	7/29 3 ♓ 01R	4/24 2 ♎ 01R	1/18 23 ♏ 00
11/21 1 ♑ 01	8/18 29 ♒ 01R	5/14 0 ♎ 01R	2/ 7 24 ♏ 01
12/11 4 ♑ 01	9/ 7 25 ♒ 01R	6/ 3 0 ♎ 00	2/27 24 ♏ 01R
12/31 8 ♑ 00	9/27 22 ♒ 00R	6/23 1 ♎ 00	3/19 24 ♏ 00R
1973	10/17 20 ♒ 00R	7/13 3 ♎ 00	4/ 8 22 ♏ 01R
1/20 11 ♑ 00	11/ 6 20 ♒ 00	8/ 2 6 ♎ 00	4/28 20 ♏ 01R
2/ 9 14 ♑ 00	11/26 22 ♒ 00	8/22 10 ♎ 00	5/18 18 ♏ 00R
3/ 1 17 ♑ 00	12/16 25 ♒ 01	9/11 13 ♎ 01	6/ 7 16 ♏ 00R
3/21 19 ♑ 00	1976	10/ 1 18 ♎ 00	6/27 14 ♏ 01R
4/10 20 ♑ 01	1/ 5 0 ♓ 00	10/21 22 ♎ 00	7/17 13 ♏ 01R
4/30 21 ♑ 00R	1/25 5 ♓ 01	11/10 26 ♎ 00	8/ 6 13 ♏ 01
5/20 20 ♑ 00R	2/14 11 ♓ 01	11/30 29 ♎ 01	8/26 14 ♏ 01
6/ 9 18 ♑ 00R	3/ 5 18 ♓ 00	12/20 2 ♏ 01	9/15 16 ♏ 00
6/29 15 ♑ 01R	3/25 24 ♓ 01	1979	10/ 5 18 ♏ 00
7/19 12 ♑ 01R	4/14 1 ♈ 00	1/ 9 4 ♏ 01	10/25 20 ♏ 01
8/ 8 10 ♑ 00R	5/ 4 7 ♈ 01	1/29 5 ♏ 01	11/14 23 ♏ 00
8/28 8 ♑ 00R	5/24 14 ♈ 00	2/18 5 ♏ 01R	12/ 4 25 ♏ 01
9/17 7 ♑ 01R	6/13 20 ♈ 01	3/10 4 ♏ 00R	12/24 27 ♏ 01
10/ 7 8 ♑ 00	7/ 3 26 ♈ 00	3/30 2 ♏ 00R	1982
10/27 9 ♑ 01	7/23 0 ♉ 01	4/19 29 ♎ 00R	1/13 0 ♐ 00
11/16 12 ♑ 00	8/12 4 ♉ 01	5/ 9 26 ♎ 00R	2/ 2 1 ♐ 01
12/ 6 15 ♑ 00	9/ 1 6 ♉ 00	5/29 23 ♎ 01R	2/22 2 ♐ 00
12/26 18 ♑ 01	9/21 5 ♉ 00R	6/18 22 ♎ 01R	3/14 2 ♐ 00R
1974	10/11 1 ♉ 00R	7/ 8 22 ♎ 01	4/ 3 1 ♐ 00R
1/15 22 ♑ 01	10/31 25 ♈ 00R	7/28 23 ♎ 00	4/23 29 ♏ 01R
2/ 4 26 ♑ 01	11/20 19 ♈ 00R	8/17 25 ♎ 00	5/13 27 ♏ 01R
2/24 0 ♒ 00	12/10 17 ♈ 00R	9/ 6 27 ♎ 00	6/ 2 25 ♏ 00R
3/16 3 ♒ 01	12/30 18 ♈ 01	9/26 0 ♏ 00	6/22 23 ♏ 00R
4/ 5 6 ♒ 00	1977	10/16 3 ♏ 00	7/12 22 ♏ 00R
4/25 8 ♒ 00	1/19 23 ♈ 01	11/ 5 6 ♏ 00	8/ 1 21 ♏ 01R
5/15 9 ♒ 00	2/ 8 1 ♉ 01	11/25 9 ♏ 00	8/21 21 ♏ 01
6/ 4 8 ♒ 01R	2/28 12 ♉ 00	12/15 12 ♏ 00	9/10 22 ♏ 01
6/24 6 ♒ 01R	3/20 24 ♉ 00	1980	9/30 24 ♏ 00
7/14 3 ♒ 01R	4/ 9 7 ♊ 01	1/ 4 14 ♏ 00	10/20 26 ♏ 01
8/ 3 0 ♒ 00R	4/29 21 ♊ 01	1/24 15 ♏ 01	11/ 9 28 ♏ 01
8/23 27 ♑ 00R	5/19 5 ♋ 01	2/13 16 ♏ 01	11/29 1 ♐ 00
9/12 24 ♑ 01R	6/ 8 19 ♋ 00	3/ 4 16 ♏ 00R	12/19 3 ♐ 01

84 *Astrological Markers of ADD and ADHD*

1983	10/ 4 16 ♐ 00	6/30 2 ♒ 01R	3/27 15 ♂ 00
1/ 8 6 ♐ 00	10/24 18 ♐ 00	7/20 29 ♑ 01R	4/16 28 ♂ 00
1/28 8 ♐ 00	11/13 20 ♐ 00	8/ 9 26 ♑ 00R	5/ 6 11 ♊ 01
2/17 9 ♐ 00	12/ 3 23 ♐ 00	8/29 23 ♑ 00R	5/26 25 ♊ 01
3/ 9 9 ♐ 01	12/23 26 ♐ 00	9/18 21 ♑ 01R	6/15 10 ♋ 00
3/29 9 ♐ 00R	**1986**	10/ 8 21 ♑ 01	7/ 5 23 ♋ 01
4/18 8 ♐ 00R	1/12 29 ♐ 00	10/28 22 ♑ 01	7/25 7 ♌ 00
5/ 8 6 ♐ 00R	2/ 1 1 ♑ 01	11/17 25 ♑ 00	8/14 19 ♌ 00
5/28 4 ♐ 00R	2/21 3 ♑ 01	12/ 7 28 ♑ 01	9/ 3 0 ♍ 01
6/17 2 ♐ 00R	3/13 5 ♑ 01	12/27 2 ♒ 01	9/23 10 ♍ 01
7/ 7 0 ♐ 00R	4/ 2 6 ♑ 00	**1989**	10/13 19 ♍ 01
7/27 29 ♏ 00R	4/22 6 ♑ 00R	1/16 7 ♒ 00	11/ 2 27 ♍ 01
8/16 28 ♏ 01	5/12 5 ♑ 00R	2/ 5 11 ♒ 01	11/22 4 ♎ 01
9/ 5 29 ♏ 01	6/ 1 3 ♑ 00R	2/25 16 ♒ 00	12/12 9 ♎ 01
9/25 0 ♐ 01	6/21 0 ♑ 01R	3/17 20 ♒ 01	**1992**
10/15 2 ♐ 01	7/11 27 ♐ 01R	4/ 6 24 ♒ 01	1/ 1 13 ♎ 00
11/ 4 4 ♐ 01	7/31 25 ♐ 01R	4/26 28 ♒ 00	1/21 14 ♎ 00R
11/24 7 ♐ 00	8/20 24 ♐ 00R	5/16 1 ♓ 00	2/10 12 ♎ 01R
12/14 9 ♐ 01	9/ 9 24 ♐ 00	6/ 5 2 ♓ 01	3/ 1 9 ♎ 00R
1984	9/29 24 ♐ 01	6/25 2 ♓ 01R	3/21 4 ♎ 01R
1/ 3 12 ♐ 00	10/19 26 ♐ 00	7/15 0 ♓ 01R	4/10 0 ♎ 00R
1/23 14 ♐ 01	11/ 8 28 ♐ 01	8/ 4 27 ♒ 01R	4/30 27 ♍ 00R
2/12 16 ♐ 00	11/28 1 ♑ 00	8/24 23 ♒ 00R	5/20 26 ♍ 00R
3/ 3 17 ♐ 00	12/18 4 ♑ 00	9/13 19 ♒ 00R	6/ 9 26 ♍ 01
3/23 17 ♐ 01R	**1987**	10/ 3 16 ♒ 01R	6/29 28 ♍ 01
4/12 16 ♐ 01R	1/ 7 7 ♑ 01	10/23 15 ♒ 01	7/19 1 ♎ 01
5/ 2 15 ♐ 01R	1/27 10 ♑ 01	11/12 17 ♒ 00	8/ 8 5 ♎ 00
5/22 13 ♐ 00R	2/16 13 ♑ 01	12/ 2 19 ♒ 01	8/28 9 ♎ 00
6/11 11 ♐ 00R	3/ 8 16 ♑ 00	12/22 23 ♒ 01	9/17 13 ♎ 01
7/ 1 9 ♐ 00R	3/28 18 ♑ 00	**1990**	10/ 7 17 ♎ 01
7/21 7 ♐ 00R	4/17 19 ♑ 00	1/11 28 ♒ 00	10/27 22 ♎ 00
8/10 6 ♐ 01R	5/ 7 18 ♑ 01R	1/31 3 ♓ 01	11/16 26 ♎ 00
8/30 6 ♐ 01	5/27 17 ♑ 01R	2/20 9 ♓ 01	12/ 6 29 ♎ 01
9/19 7 ♐ 00	6/16 15 ♑ 00R	3/12 16 ♓ 00	12/26 2 ♏ 00
10/ 9 9 ♐ 00	7/ 6 12 ♑ 01R	4/ 1 22 ♓ 00	**1993**
10/29 11 ♐ 00	7/26 9 ♑ 01R	4/21 28 ♓ 01	1/15 4 ♏ 00
11/18 13 ♐ 01	8/15 7 ♑ 00R	5/11 4 ♈ 01	2/ 4 4 ♏ 01
12/ 8 16 ♐ 00	9/ 4 5 ♑ 01R	5/31 10 ♈ 01	2/24 4 ♏ 00R
12/28 18 ♐ 01	9/24 5 ♑ 01	6/20 15 ♈ 01	3/16 2 ♏ 01R
1985	10/14 6 ♑ 01	7/10 20 ♈ 00	4/ 5 29 ♎ 01R
1/17 21 ♐ 00	11/ 3 8 ♑ 01	7/30 23 ♈ 00	4/25 26 ♎ 01R
2/ 6 23 ♐ 01	11/23 11 ♑ 01	8/19 24 ♈ 00	5/15 23 ♎ 01R
2/26 25 ♐ 00	12/13 14 ♑ 01	9/ 8 23 ♈ 00R	6/ 4 21 ♎ 01R
3/18 26 ♐ 00	**1988**	9/28 19 ♈ 00R	6/24 21 ♎ 00R
4/ 7 26 ♐ 00R	1/ 2 18 ♑ 00	10/18 13 ♈ 00R	7/14 21 ♎ 00
4/27 25 ♐ 00R	1/22 22 ♑ 00	11/ 7 7 ♈ 01R	8/ 3 22 ♎ 01
5/17 23 ♐ 01R	2/11 25 ♑ 01	11/27 5 ♈ 00R	8/23 24 ♎ 01
6/ 6 21 ♐ 00R	3/ 2 29 ♑ 00	12/17 5 ♈ 01	9/12 27 ♎ 00
6/26 18 ♐ 01R	3/22 2 ♒ 00	**1991**	10/ 2 0 ♏ 00
7/16 16 ♐ 01R	4/11 4 ♒ 01	1/ 6 9 ♈ 01	10/22 3 ♏ 00
8/ 5 15 ♐ 00R	5/ 1 6 ♒ 00	1/26 15 ♈ 01	11/11 6 ♏ 01
8/25 14 ♐ 01R	5/21 6 ♒ 00R	2/15 24 ♈ 00	12/ 1 9 ♏ 01
9/14 15 ♐ 00	6/10 5 ♒ 00R	3/ 7 4 ♂ 00	12/21 12 ♏ 00

Hidalgo Tables

Date	Pos	Date	Pos	Date	Pos	Date	Pos
1994		10/ 6	24 ♏ 01	7/ 3	17 ♐ 01R	3/29	4 ♒ 00
1/10	14 ♏ 00	10/26	26 ♏ 01	7/23	15 ♐ 01R	4/18	6 ♒ 01
1/30	15 ♏ 00	11/15	29 ♏ 00	8/12	14 ♐ 00R	5/ 8	7 ♒ 01
2/19	15 ♏ 01R	12/ 5	1 ♐ 01	9/ 1	14 ♐ 00	5/28	7 ♒ 01R
3/11	15 ♏ 00R	12/25	4 ♐ 00	9/21	14 ♐ 01	6/17	6 ♒ 00R
3/31	13 ♏ 00R	1997		10/11	16 ♐ 00	7/ 7	3 ♒ 00R
4/20	11 ♏ 00R	1/14	6 ♐ 00	10/31	18 ♐ 00	7/27	29 ♑ 01R
5/10	8 ♏ 00R	2/ 3	8 ♐ 00	11/20	20 ♐ 01	8/16	26 ♑ 00R
5/30	6 ♏ 00R	2/23	9 ♐ 00	12/10	23 ♐ 01	9/ 5	23 ♑ 01R
6/19	4 ♏ 00R	3/15	9 ♐ 00R	12/30	26 ♐ 01	9/25	22 ♑ 01R
7/ 9	3 ♏ 01R	4/ 4	8 ♐ 01R	2000		10/15	22 ♑ 01
7/29	3 ♏ 01	4/24	7 ♐ 00R	1/19	29 ♐ 01	11/ 4	24 ♑ 01
8/18	4 ♏ 01	5/14	5 ♐ 00R	2/ 8	2 ♑ 00	11/24	27 ♑ 00
9/ 7	6 ♏ 01	6/ 3	2 ♐ 01R	2/28	4 ♑ 00	12/14	1 ♒ 00
9/27	8 ♏ 01	6/23	0 ♐ 01R	3/19	5 ♑ 01	2003	
10/17	11 ♏ 01	7/13	29 ♏ 00R	4/ 8	6 ♑ 00	1/ 3	5 ♒ 00
11/ 6	14 ♏ 00	8/ 2	28 ♏ 00R	4/28	5 ♑ 01R	1/23	10 ♒ 00
11/26	16 ♏ 01	8/22	28 ♏ 00	5/18	4 ♑ 00R	2/12	15 ♒ 00
12/16	19 ♏ 01	9/11	29 ♏ 00	6/ 7	2 ♑ 00R	3/ 4	19 ♒ 01
1995		10/ 1	0 ♐ 01	6/27	29 ♐ 00R	3/24	24 ♒ 01
1/ 5	21 ♏ 01	10/21	2 ♐ 01	7/17	26 ♐ 01R	4/13	28 ♒ 01
1/25	23 ♏ 00	11/10	5 ♐ 00	8/ 6	24 ♐ 01R	5/ 3	2 ♓ 01
2/14	24 ♏ 00	11/30	7 ♐ 01	8/26	23 ♐ 01R	5/23	5 ♓ 00
3/ 6	24 ♏ 00R	12/20	10 ♐ 00	9/15	23 ♐ 01	6/12	6 ♓ 01
3/26	23 ♏ 00R	1998		10/ 5	24 ♐ 01	7/ 2	6 ♓ 01R
4/15	21 ♏ 00R	1/ 9	12 ♐ 01	10/25	26 ♐ 01	7/22	4 ♓ 01R
5/ 5	19 ♏ 00R	1/29	14 ♐ 01	11/14	29 ♐ 00	8/11	1 ♓ 00R
5/25	16 ♏ 01R	2/18	16 ♐ 00	12/ 4	2 ♑ 00	8/31	26 ♒ 01R
6/14	14 ♏ 01R	3/10	17 ♐ 00	12/24	5 ♑ 00	9/20	22 ♒ 01R
7/ 4	13 ♏ 00R	3/30	16 ♐ 01R	2001		10/10	20 ♒ 00R
7/24	12 ♏ 01R	4/19	16 ♐ 00R	1/13	8 ♑ 01	10/30	19 ♒ 01
8/13	13 ♏ 00	5/ 9	14 ♐ 00R	2/ 2	12 ♑ 00	11/19	21 ♒ 00
9/ 2	14 ♏ 00	5/29	12 ♐ 00R	2/22	14 ♑ 01	12/ 9	24 ♒ 00
9/22	16 ♏ 00	6/18	9 ♐ 01R	3/14	17 ♑ 00	12/29	28 ♒ 01
10/12	18 ♏ 00	7/ 8	7 ♐ 01R	4/ 3	18 ♑ 01	2004	
11/ 1	20 ♏ 01	7/28	6 ♐ 00R	4/23	19 ♑ 00	1/18	4 ♓ 00
11/21	23 ♏ 00	8/17	5 ♐ 01R	5/13	19 ♑ 00R	2/ 7	10 ♓ 00
12/11	25 ♏ 01	9/ 6	6 ♐ 00	6/ 2	17 ♑ 00R	2/27	16 ♓ 01
12/31	28 ♏ 00	9/26	7 ♐ 00	6/22	14 ♑ 01R	3/18	23 ♓ 00
1996		10/16	9 ♐ 00	7/12	11 ♑ 01R	4/ 7	0 ♈ 00
1/20	0 ♐ 00	11/ 5	11 ♐ 00	8/ 1	8 ♑ 01R	4/27	7 ♈ 00
2/ 9	1 ♐ 00	11/25	14 ♐ 00	8/21	6 ♑ 01R	5/17	14 ♈ 00
2/29	1 ♐ 01	12/15	16 ♐ 01	9/10	5 ♑ 01R	6/ 6	21 ♈ 00
3/20	1 ♐ 00R	1999		9/30	6 ♑ 00	6/26	27 ♈ 01
4/ 9	0 ♐ 00R	1/ 4	19 ♐ 00	10/20	7 ♑ 00	7/16	3 ♉ 01
4/29	28 ♏ 00R	1/24	21 ♐ 01	11/ 9	9 ♑ 01	8/ 5	8 ♉ 01
5/19	26 ♏ 00R	2/13	23 ♐ 01	11/29	12 ♑ 01	8/25	12 ♉ 00
6/ 8	23 ♏ 01R	3/ 5	25 ♐ 00	12/19	16 ♑ 00	9/14	13 ♉ 01
6/28	22 ♏ 00R	3/25	25 ♐ 01	2002		10/ 4	12 ♉ 01R
7/18	21 ♏ 00R	4/14	25 ♐ 01R	1/ 8	20 ♑ 00	10/24	7 ♉ 01R
8/ 7	20 ♏ 01	5/ 4	24 ♐ 00R	1/28	24 ♑ 00	11/13	1 ♉ 00R
8/27	21 ♏ 00	5/24	22 ♐ 00R	2/17	27 ♑ 01	12/ 3	25 ♈ 01R
9/16	22 ♏ 01	6/13	19 ♐ 01R	3/ 9	1 ♒ 00	12/23	24 ♈ 01

2005	10/ 9 3 ♏ 01	7/ 5 23 ♏ 01R	3/31 28 ♐ 00R
1/12 28 ♈ 01	10/29 6 ♏ 01	7/25 22 ♏ 01R	4/20 27 ♐ 01R
2/ 1 6 ♉ 01	11/18 9 ♏ 01	8/14 22 ♏ 01	5/10 26 ♐ 01R
2/21 17 ♉ 00	12/ 8 12 ♏ 01	9/ 3 23 ♏ 01	5/30 24 ♐ 00R
3/13 29 ♉ 01	12/28 15 ♏ 00	9/23 25 ♏ 00	6/19 21 ♐ 01R
4/ 2 13 ♊ 01	2008	10/13 26 ♏ 01	7/ 9 19 ♐ 00R
4/22 28 ♊ 00	1/17 16 ♏ 01	11/ 2 29 ♏ 00	7/29 17 ♐ 01R
5/12 11 ♋ 01	2/ 6 17 ♏ 01	11/22 1 ♐ 01	8/18 16 ♐ 01R
6/ 1 25 ♋ 00	2/26 17 ♏ 01R	12/12 4 ♐ 00	9/ 7 16 ♐ 01
6/21 7 ♌ 00	3/17 17 ♏ 00R	2011	9/27 17 ♐ 00
7/11 18 ♌ 00	4/ 6 15 ♏ 00R	1/ 1 6 ♐ 01	10/17 19 ♐ 00
7/31 28 ♌ 01	4/26 12 ♏ 01R	1/21 8 ♐ 01	11/ 6 21 ♐ 00
8/20 8 ♍ 00	5/16 10 ♏ 00R	2/10 10 ♐ 00	11/26 24 ♐ 00
9/ 9 16 ♍ 01	6/ 5 8 ♏ 00R	3/ 2 11 ♐ 00	12/16 27 ♐ 00
9/29 24 ♍ 01	6/25 6 ♏ 01R	3/22 11 ♐ 00R	2014
10/19 1 ♎ 01	7/15 6 ♏ 00R	4/11 10 ♐ 00R	1/ 5 0 ♑ 00
11/ 8 8 ♎ 00	8/ 4 6 ♏ 00	5/ 1 8 ♐ 01R	1/25 2 ♑ 01
11/28 13 ♎ 00	8/24 7 ♏ 01	5/21 6 ♐ 01R	2/14 5 ♑ 01
12/18 17 ♎ 01	9/13 9 ♏ 00	6/10 4 ♐ 00R	3/ 6 7 ♑ 01
2006	10/ 3 11 ♏ 01	6/30 2 ♐ 00R	3/26 8 ♑ 01
1/ 7 20 ♎ 00	10/23 14 ♏ 00	7/20 0 ♐ 01R	4/15 9 ♑ 00R
1/27 20 ♎ 01R	11/12 17 ♏ 00	8/ 9 0 ♐ 00R	5/ 5 8 ♑ 01R
2/16 19 ♎ 01R	12/ 2 19 ♏ 01	8/29 0 ♐ 01	5/25 6 ♑ 01R
3/ 8 16 ♎ 01R	12/22 22 ♏ 00	9/18 1 ♐ 01	6/14 4 ♑ 01R
3/28 12 ♎ 01R	2009	10/ 8 3 ♐ 00	7/ 4 1 ♑ 01R
4/17 8 ♎ 00R	1/11 24 ♏ 00	10/28 5 ♐ 00	7/24 29 ♐ 00R
5/ 7 5 ♎ 00R	1/31 25 ♏ 01	11/17 7 ♐ 01	8/13 27 ♐ 00R
5/27 4 ♎ 00R	2/20 26 ♏ 00	12/ 7 10 ♐ 00	9/ 2 26 ♐ 00R
6/16 4 ♎ 00	3/12 25 ♏ 01R	12/27 12 ♐ 01	9/22 26 ♐ 01
7/ 6 5 ♎ 01	4/ 1 24 ♏ 01R	2012	10/12 27 ♐ 01
7/26 8 ♎ 00	4/21 22 ♏ 01R	1/16 15 ♐ 00	11/ 1 0 ♑ 00
8/15 11 ♎ 00	5/11 20 ♏ 01R	2/ 5 17 ♐ 00	11/21 2 ♑ 01
9/ 4 14 ♎ 01	5/31 18 ♏ 00R	2/25 18 ♐ 01	12/11 5 ♑ 01
9/24 18 ♎ 01	6/20 16 ♏ 00R	3/16 19 ♐ 00	12/31 9 ♑ 00
10/14 22 ♎ 01	7/10 15 ♏ 00R	4/ 5 19 ♐ 00R	2015
11/ 3 26 ♎ 01	7/30 14 ♏ 01	4/25 17 ♐ 01R	1/20 12 ♑ 01
11/23 0 ♏ 00	8/19 15 ♏ 01	5/15 16 ♐ 00R	2/ 9 16 ♑ 00
12/13 3 ♏ 00	9/ 8 16 ♏ 01	6/ 4 13 ♐ 01R	3/ 1 18 ♑ 01
2007	9/28 18 ♏ 01	6/24 11 ♐ 00R	3/21 21 ♑ 00
1/ 2 5 ♏ 01	10/18 20 ♏ 01	7/14 9 ♐ 00R	4/10 22 ♑ 01
1/22 7 ♏ 00	11/ 7 23 ♏ 00	8/ 3 8 ♐ 00R	4/30 23 ♑ 00R
2/11 7 ♏ 01R	11/27 25 ♏ 01	8/23 7 ♐ 01	5/20 22 ♑ 01R
3/ 3 7 ♏ 00R	12/17 28 ♏ 00	9/12 8 ♐ 00	6/ 9 20 ♑ 01R
3/23 5 ♏ 00R	2010	10/ 2 9 ♐ 01	6/29 18 ♑ 00R
4/12 2 ♏ 00R	1/ 6 0 ♐ 01	10/22 11 ♐ 01	7/19 15 ♑ 00R
5/ 2 29 ♎ 00R	1/26 2 ♐ 00	11/11 14 ♐ 00	8/ 8 12 ♑ 00R
5/22 26 ♎ 01R	2/15 3 ♐ 00	12/ 1 16 ♐ 01	8/28 10 ♑ 00R
6/11 25 ♎ 00R	3/ 7 3 ♐ 01R	12/21 19 ♐ 01	9/17 9 ♑ 00R
7/ 1 24 ♎ 00R	3/27 3 ♐ 00R	2013	10/ 7 9 ♑ 01
7/21 24 ♎ 01	4/16 1 ♐ 01R	1/10 22 ♐ 00	10/27 11 ♑ 00
8/10 26 ♎ 00	5/ 6 29 ♏ 01R	1/30 24 ♐ 01	11/16 14 ♑ 00
8/30 28 ♎ 00	5/26 27 ♏ 01R	2/19 26 ♐ 01	12/ 6 17 ♑ 00
9/19 0 ♏ 01	6/15 25 ♏ 00R	3/11 27 ♐ 01	12/26 21 ♑ 00

Hidalgo Tables 87

2016	10/11 8 ♋ 00	7/ 7 27 ♎ 01	4/ 2 4 ♐ 01R
1/15 25 ♑ 00	10/31 18 ♋ 00	7/27 28 ♎ 00	4/22 3 ♐ 00R
2/ 4 29 ♑ 00	11/20 26 ♋ 01	8/16 29 ♎ 01	5/12 1 ♐ 00R
2/24 3 ♒ 00	12/10 1 ♌ 00	9/ 5 1 ♏ 01	6/ 1 28 ♏ 01R
3/15 6 ♒ 01	12/30 29 ♋ 01R	9/25 4 ♏ 00	6/21 26 ♏ 01R
4/ 4 9 ♒ 01	2019	10/15 7 ♏ 00	7/11 25 ♏ 00R
4/24 12 ♒ 00	1/19 24 ♋ 00R	11/ 4 9 ♏ 01	7/31 24 ♏ 01R
5/14 13 ♒ 01	2/ 8 20 ♋ 01R	11/24 12 ♏ 01	8/20 24 ♏ 01
6/ 3 13 ♒ 00R	2/28 21 ♋ 01	12/14 15 ♏ 01	9/ 9 25 ♏ 01
6/23 11 ♒ 01R	3/20 26 ♋ 00	2022	9/29 27 ♏ 00
7/13 8 ♒ 01R	4/ 9 2 ♌ 00	1/ 3 17 ♏ 01	10/19 29 ♏ 00
8/ 2 5 ♒ 00R	4/29 9 ♌ 00	1/23 19 ♏ 00	11/ 8 1 ♐ 01
8/22 1 ♒ 01R	5/19 16 ♌ 01	2/12 20 ♏ 00	11/28 4 ♐ 00
9/11 28 ♑ 01R	6/ 8 24 ♌ 00	3/ 4 19 ♏ 01R	12/18 6 ♐ 01
10/ 1 27 ♑ 01R	6/28 1 ♍ 01	3/24 18 ♏ 01R	2025
10/21 28 ♑ 00	7/18 8 ♍ 01	4/13 16 ♏ 01R	1/ 7 9 ♐ 00
11/10 0 ♒ 00	8/ 7 15 ♍ 01	5/ 3 14 ♏ 01R	1/27 11 ♐ 00
11/30 3 ♒ 00	8/27 22 ♍ 01	5/23 12 ♏ 00R	2/16 12 ♐ 01
12/20 7 ♒ 00	9/16 29 ♍ 00	6/12 10 ♏ 00R	3/ 8 13 ♐ 00
2017	10/ 6 5 ♎ 01	7/ 2 8 ♏ 01R	3/28 13 ♐ 00R
1/ 9 11 ♒ 01	10/26 11 ♎ 00	7/22 8 ♏ 00	4/17 11 ♐ 01R
1/29 16 ♒ 01	11/15 16 ♎ 00	8/11 9 ♏ 00	5/ 7 10 ♐ 00R
2/18 22 ♒ 00	12/ 5 20 ♎ 01	8/31 10 ♏ 00	5/27 7 ♐ 01R
3/10 27 ♒ 00	12/25 24 ♎ 00	9/20 12 ♏ 00	6/16 5 ♐ 01R
3/30 2 ♓ 00	2020	10/10 14 ♏ 00	7/ 6 3 ♐ 01R
4/19 7 ♓ 00	1/14 26 ♎ 00	10/30 17 ♏ 00	7/26 2 ♐ 01R
5/ 9 11 ♓ 00	2/ 3 26 ♎ 01R	11/19 19 ♏ 01	8/15 2 ♐ 00
5/29 14 ♓ 01	2/23 25 ♎ 00R	12/ 9 22 ♏ 00	9/ 4 2 ♐ 01
6/18 16 ♓ 01	3/14 22 ♎ 01R	12/29 24 ♏ 01	9/24 3 ♐ 01
7/ 8 16 ♓ 01R	4/ 3 18 ♎ 01R	2023	10/14 5 ♐ 01
7/28 15 ♓ 00R	4/23 15 ♎ 00R	1/18 26 ♏ 00	11/ 3 7 ♐ 01
8/17 11 ♓ 01R	5/13 12 ♎ 00R	2/ 7 27 ♏ 01	11/23 10 ♐ 00
9/ 6 7 ♓ 00R	6/ 2 10 ♎ 01R	2/27 28 ♏ 00R	12/13 12 ♐ 01
9/26 2 ♓ 01R	6/22 10 ♎ 01	3/19 27 ♏ 01R	2026
10/16 29 ♒ 01R	7/12 12 ♎ 00	4/ 8 26 ♏ 00R	1/ 2 15 ♐ 01
11/ 5 29 ♒ 00	8/ 1 14 ♎ 00	4/28 24 ♏ 00R	1/22 17 ♐ 01
11/25 0 ♓ 01	8/21 16 ♎ 01	5/18 22 ♏ 00R	2/11 19 ♐ 01
12/15 3 ♓ 01	9/10 20 ♎ 00	6/ 7 19 ♏ 01R	3/ 3 21 ♐ 00
2018	9/30 23 ♎ 01	6/27 18 ♏ 00R	3/23 21 ♐ 00
1/ 4 8 ♓ 01	10/20 27 ♎ 00	7/17 17 ♏ 00R	4/12 21 ♐ 00R
1/24 14 ♓ 00	11/ 9 0 ♏ 01	8/ 6 17 ♏ 00	5/ 2 19 ♐ 01R
2/13 20 ♓ 01	11/29 4 ♏ 00	8/26 17 ♏ 01	5/22 17 ♐ 01R
3/ 5 28 ♓ 00	12/19 7 ♏ 00	9/15 19 ♏ 00	6/11 15 ♐ 00R
3/25 5 ♈ 01	2021	10/ 5 21 ♏ 00	7/ 1 12 ♐ 01R
4/14 13 ♈ 01	1/ 8 9 ♏ 00	10/25 23 ♏ 00	7/21 11 ♐ 00R
5/ 4 22 ♈ 00	1/28 10 ♏ 01	11/14 25 ♏ 01	8/10 10 ♐ 00R
5/24 0 ♉ 01	2/17 10 ♏ 01R	12/ 4 28 ♏ 00	8/30 10 ♐ 00
6/13 9 ♉ 00	3/ 9 9 ♏ 01R	12/24 0 ♐ 01	9/19 10 ♐ 01
7/ 3 18 ♉ 01	3/29 7 ♏ 01R	2024	10/ 9 12 ♐ 00
7/23 27 ♉ 01	4/18 4 ♏ 01R	1/13 2 ♐ 01	10/29 14 ♐ 00
8/12 7 ♊ 01	5/ 8 2 ♏ 00R	2/ 2 4 ♐ 01	11/18 16 ♐ 01
9/ 1 17 ♊ 01	5/28 29 ♎ 01R	2/22 5 ♐ 00	12/ 8 19 ♐ 01
9/21 27 ♊ 01	6/17 28 ♎ 00R	3/13 5 ♐ 01R	12/28 22 ♐ 00

2027	10/13 14 ♑ 00	7/ 9 20 ♊ 01	4/ 5 10 ♏ 00R
1/17 25 ♐ 00	11/ 2 16 ♑ 00	7/29 4 ♋ 01	4/25 7 ♏ 00R
2/ 6 27 ♐ 01	11/22 18 ♑ 01	8/18 19 ♋ 00	5/15 4 ♏ 01R
2/26 29 ♐ 00	12/12 22 ♑ 00	9/ 7 3 ♌ 01	6/ 4 2 ♏ 01R
3/18 0 ♑ 01	2030	9/27 17 ♌ 01	6/24 1 ♏ 00R
4/ 7 0 ♑ 01R	1/ 1 26 ♑ 00	10/17 0 ♍ 00	7/14 0 ♏ 01
4/27 0 ♑ 00R	1/21 0 ♒ 01	11/ 6 11 ♍ 00	8/ 3 1 ♏ 01
5/17 28 ♐ 01R	2/10 5 ♒ 00	11/26 20 ♍ 00	8/23 2 ♏ 01
6/ 6 26 ♐ 00R	3/ 2 9 ♒ 00	12/16 26 ♍ 00	9/12 4 ♏ 01
6/26 23 ♐ 01R	3/22 13 ♒ 00	2033	10/ 2 7 ♏ 00
7/16 21 ♐ 00R	4/11 16 ♒ 01	1/ 5 29 ♍ 00	10/22 10 ♏ 00
8/ 5 19 ♐ 01R	5/ 1 19 ♒ 00	1/25 28 ♍ 00R	11/11 13 ♏ 00
8/25 18 ♐ 01R	5/21 20 ♒ 01	2/14 23 ♍ 01R	12/ 1 15 ♏ 01
9/14 19 ♐ 00	6/10 20 ♒ 01R	3/ 6 17 ♍ 01R	12/21 18 ♏ 00
10/ 4 20 ♐ 00	6/30 19 ♒ 00R	3/26 12 ♍ 00R	2036
10/24 21 ♐ 01	7/20 16 ♒ 00R	4/15 9 ♍ 01R	1/10 20 ♏ 00
11/13 24 ♐ 00	8/ 9 12 ♒ 00R	5/ 5 9 ♍ 00	1/30 21 ♏ 01
12/ 3 27 ♐ 00	8/29 8 ♒ 00R	5/25 11 ♍ 00	2/19 22 ♏ 00
12/23 0 ♑ 00	9/18 5 ♒ 01R	6/14 14 ♍ 01	3/10 21 ♏ 01R
2028	10/ 8 4 ♒ 00R	7/ 4 18 ♍ 01	3/30 20 ♏ 01R
1/12 3 ♑ 00	10/28 4 ♒ 01	7/24 23 ♍ 01	4/19 18 ♏ 01R
2/ 1 6 ♑ 00	11/17 7 ♒ 00	8/13 28 ♍ 01	5/ 9 16 ♏ 00R
2/21 9 ♑ 00	12/ 7 10 ♒ 00	9/ 2 3 ♎ 01	5/29 13 ♏ 01R
3/12 11 ♑ 00	12/27 14 ♒ 01	9/22 8 ♎ 01	6/18 12 ♏ 00R
4/ 1 12 ♑ 00	2031	10/12 13 ♎ 01	7/ 8 11 ♏ 00R
4/21 12 ♑ 01R	1/16 19 ♒ 01	11/ 1 18 ♎ 01	7/28 10 ♏ 01
5/11 11 ♑ 01R	2/ 5 25 ♒ 00	11/21 23 ♎ 00	8/17 11 ♏ 01
5/31 9 ♑ 01R	2/25 0 ♓ 01	12/11 26 ♎ 01	9/ 6 12 ♏ 01
6/20 7 ♑ 00R	3/17 6 ♓ 01	12/31 29 ♎ 00	9/26 14 ♏ 01
7/10 4 ♑ 00R	4/ 6 12 ♓ 00	2034	10/16 17 ♏ 00
7/30 1 ♑ 01R	4/26 17 ♓ 00	1/20 0 ♏ 01	11/ 5 19 ♏ 01
8/19 0 ♑ 00R	5/16 22 ♓ 00	2/ 9 1 ♏ 00R	11/25 22 ♏ 00
9/ 8 29 ♐ 00R	6/ 5 26 ♓ 00	3/ 1 29 ♎ 01R	12/15 24 ♏ 01
9/28 29 ♐ 01	6/25 29 ♓ 00	3/21 27 ♎ 00R	2037
10/18 1 ♑ 00	7/15 0 ♈ 01	4/10 24 ♎ 00R	1/ 4 27 ♏ 00
11/ 7 3 ♑ 01	8/ 4 0 ♈ 00R	4/30 20 ♎ 01R	1/24 28 ♏ 01
11/27 6 ♑ 01	8/24 27 ♓ 00R	5/20 18 ♎ 00R	2/13 29 ♏ 01
12/17 9 ♑ 01	9/13 22 ♓ 01R	6/ 9 16 ♎ 01R	3/ 5 29 ♏ 01R
2029	10/ 3 17 ♓ 00R	6/29 16 ♎ 01	3/25 29 ♏ 00R
1/ 6 13 ♑ 00	10/23 13 ♓ 01R	7/19 17 ♎ 01	4/14 27 ♏ 01R
1/26 17 ♑ 00	11/12 12 ♓ 00R	8/ 8 19 ♎ 00	5/ 4 25 ♏ 01R
2/15 20 ♑ 00	12/ 2 13 ♓ 00	8/28 21 ♎ 01	5/24 23 ♏ 00R
3/ 7 23 ♑ 00	12/22 16 ♓ 01	9/17 24 ♎ 01	6/13 21 ♏ 00R
3/27 25 ♑ 01	2032	10/ 7 28 ♎ 00	7/ 3 19 ♏ 01R
4/16 27 ♑ 00	1/11 21 ♓ 01	10/27 1 ♏ 01	7/23 19 ♏ 00R
5/ 6 27 ♑ 01R	1/31 28 ♓ 00	11/16 4 ♏ 01	8/12 19 ♏ 00
5/26 27 ♑ 00R	2/20 5 ♈ 01	12/ 6 7 ♏ 01	9/ 1 19 ♏ 01
6/15 25 ♑ 00R	3/11 14 ♈ 00	12/26 10 ♏ 01	9/21 21 ♏ 00
7/ 5 22 ♑ 00R	3/31 23 ♈ 01	2035	10/11 23 ♏ 00
7/25 18 ♑ 01R	4/20 3 ♉ 00	1/15 12 ♏ 00	10/31 25 ♏ 01
8/14 16 ♑ 00R	5/10 13 ♉ 01	2/ 4 13 ♏ 00	11/20 28 ♏ 00
9/ 3 14 ♑ 00R	5/30 25 ♉ 00	2/24 13 ♏ 00R	12/10 0 ♐ 01
9/23 13 ♑ 00	6/19 7 ♊ 01	3/16 12 ♏ 00R	12/30 3 ♐ 00

Hidalgo Tables

2038	10/15 14 ♐ 01	7/12 25 ♑ 01R	4/ 7 10 ♉ 01
1/19 5 ♐ 00	11/ 4 16 ♐ 01	8/ 1 22 ♑ 00R	4/27 22 ♉ 01
2/ 8 6 ♐ 01	11/24 19 ♐ 01	8/21 19 ♑ 00R	5/17 5 ♊ 01
2/28 7 ♐ 00	12/14 22 ♐ 00	9/10 17 ♑ 01R	6/ 6 19 ♊ 01
3/20 7 ♐ 00R	2041	9/30 17 ♑ 00	6/26 4 ♋ 00
4/ 9 6 ♐ 00R	1/ 3 25 ♐ 00	10/20 18 ♑ 00	7/16 18 ♋ 01
4/29 4 ♐ 01R	1/23 28 ♐ 00	11/ 9 20 ♑ 00	8/ 5 2 ♌ 01
5/19 2 ♐ 00R	2/12 0 ♑ 00	11/29 23 ♑ 00	8/25 16 ♌ 00
6/ 8 0 ♐ 00R	3/ 4 2 ♑ 00	12/19 27 ♑ 00	9/14 28 ♌ 00
6/28 28 ♏ 00R	3/24 3 ♑ 00	2044	10/ 4 9 ♍ 00
7/18 27 ♏ 00R	4/13 3 ♑ 00R	1/ 8 1 ♒ 00	10/24 18 ♍ 01
8/ 7 26 ♏ 00R	5/ 3 2 ♑ 00R	1/28 5 ♒ 01	11/13 27 ♍ 00
8/27 26 ♏ 01	5/23 0 ♑ 01R	2/17 10 ♒ 00	12/ 3 3 ♎ 01
9/16 27 ♏ 01	6/12 28 ♐ 00R	3/ 8 14 ♒ 01	12/23 7 ♎ 01
10/ 6 29 ♏ 01	7/ 2 25 ♐ 01R	3/28 18 ♒ 01	2047
10/26 1 ♐ 01	7/22 23 ♐ 00R	4/17 22 ♒ 00	1/12 10 ♎ 00
11/15 4 ♐ 00	8/11 21 ♐ 01R	5/ 7 24 ♒ 01	2/ 1 9 ♎ 00R
12/ 5 6 ♐ 01	8/31 21 ♐ 00R	5/27 26 ♒ 01	2/21 6 ♎ 00R
12/25 9 ♐ 00	9/20 21 ♐ 00	6/16 26 ♒ 01R	3/13 1 ♎ 00R
2039	10/10 22 ♐ 01	7/ 6 25 ♒ 00R	4/ 2 25 ♍ 01R
1/14 11 ♐ 01	10/30 24 ♐ 01	7/26 21 ♒ 01R	4/22 22 ♍ 01R
2/ 3 13 ♐ 00	11/19 27 ♐ 00	8/15 17 ♒ 01R	5/12 21 ♍ 00R
2/23 14 ♐ 01	12/ 9 0 ♑ 00	9/ 4 13 ♒ 01R	6/ 1 21 ♍ 01
3/15 15 ♐ 00	12/29 3 ♑ 01	9/24 11 ♒ 00R	6/21 23 ♍ 01
4/ 4 14 ♐ 01R	2042	10/14 10 ♒ 00R	7/11 27 ♍ 00
4/24 13 ♐ 01R	1/18 6 ♑ 01	11/ 3 10 ♒ 01	7/31 0 ♎ 01
5/14 11 ♐ 01R	2/ 7 9 ♑ 01	11/23 13 ♒ 00	8/20 5 ♎ 00
6/ 3 9 ♐ 00R	2/27 12 ♑ 00	12/13 16 ♒ 01	9/ 9 9 ♎ 01
6/23 7 ♐ 00R	3/19 14 ♑ 00	2045	9/29 14 ♎ 00
7/13 5 ♐ 00R	4/ 8 15 ♑ 00	1/ 2 21 ♒ 00	10/19 18 ♎ 01
8/ 2 4 ♐ 00R	4/28 15 ♑ 00R	1/22 26 ♒ 01	11/ 8 23 ♎ 00
8/22 4 ♐ 00	5/18 14 ♑ 00R	2/11 2 ♓ 00	11/28 26 ♎ 01
9/11 4 ♐ 01	6/ 7 12 ♑ 00R	3/ 3 8 ♓ 00	12/18 0 ♏ 00
10/ 1 5 ♐ 01	6/27 9 ♑ 01R	3/23 14 ♓ 01	2048
10/21 7 ♐ 01	7/17 6 ♑ 01R	4/12 20 ♓ 01	1/ 7 2 ♏ 00
11/10 10 ♐ 00	8/ 6 4 ♑ 00R	5/ 2 26 ♓ 00	1/27 3 ♏ 01
11/30 12 ♐ 01	8/26 2 ♑ 01R	5/22 1 ♈ 01	2/16 3 ♏ 00R
12/20 15 ♐ 01	9/15 2 ♑ 00	6/11 6 ♈ 01	3/ 7 2 ♏ 00R
2040	10/ 5 2 ♑ 01	7/ 1 10 ♈ 00	3/27 29 ♎ 00R
1/ 9 18 ♐ 00	10/25 4 ♑ 01	7/21 12 ♈ 01	4/16 26 ♎ 00R
1/29 20 ♐ 00	11/14 7 ♑ 00	8/10 13 ♈ 00R	5/ 6 23 ♎ 00R
2/18 22 ♐ 00	12/ 4 10 ♑ 00	8/30 11 ♈ 00R	5/26 20 ♎ 01R
3/ 9 23 ♐ 00	12/24 13 ♑ 01	9/19 6 ♈ 01R	6/15 19 ♎ 01R
3/29 23 ♐ 01R	2043	10/ 9 1 ♈ 00R	7/ 5 19 ♎ 01
4/18 22 ♐ 01R	1/13 17 ♑ 00	10/29 26 ♓ 00R	7/25 20 ♎ 01
5/ 8 21 ♐ 00R	2/ 2 21 ♑ 00	11/18 24 ♓ 00R	8/14 22 ♎ 01
5/28 19 ♐ 00R	2/22 24 ♑ 01	12/ 8 24 ♓ 01	9/ 3 25 ♎ 00
6/17 16 ♐ 01R	3/14 27 ♑ 01	12/28 28 ♓ 00	9/23 28 ♎ 00
7/ 7 14 ♐ 01R	4/ 3 0 ♒ 00	2046	10/13 1 ♏ 00
7/27 12 ♐ 01R	4/23 1 ♒ 01	1/17 3 ♈ 01	11/ 2 4 ♏ 00
8/16 12 ♐ 00R	5/13 1 ♒ 01R	2/ 6 11 ♈ 00	11/22 7 ♏ 01
9/ 5 12 ♐ 00	6/ 2 1 ♒ 00R	2/26 19 ♈ 01	12/12 10 ♏ 00
9/25 13 ♐ 00	6/22 28 ♑ 01R	3/18 29 ♈ 01	

2049	9/28 23 ♏ 00	6/24 17 ♐ 00R	3/20 0 ♒ 01
1/ 1 12 ♏ 01	10/18 25 ♏ 00	7/14 15 ♐ 00R	4/ 9 2 ♒ 01
1/21 14 ♏ 00	11/ 7 27 ♏ 01	8/ 3 13 ♐ 01R	4/29 4 ♒ 00
2/10 14 ♏ 01	11/27 0 ♐ 00	8/23 13 ♐ 00R	5/19 4 ♒ 00R
3/ 2 14 ♏ 01R	12/17 2 ♐ 01	9/12 13 ♐ 01	6/ 8 3 ♒ 00R
3/22 13 ♏ 00R	2052	10/ 2 14 ♐ 01	6/28 0 ♒ 01R
4/11 11 ♏ 00R	1/ 6 4 ♐ 01	10/22 16 ♐ 01	7/18 27 ♑ 00R
5/ 1 8 ♏ 00R	1/26 6 ♐ 01	11/11 18 ♐ 01	8/ 7 24 ♑ 00R
5/21 5 ♏ 01R	2/15 8 ♐ 00	12/ 1 21 ♐ 01	8/27 21 ♑ 00R
6/10 4 ♏ 00R	3/ 6 8 ♐ 01	12/21 24 ♐ 01	9/16 19 ♑ 01R
6/30 2 ♏ 01R	3/26 8 ♐ 00R	2055	10/ 6 19 ♑ 01
7/20 2 ♏ 01	4/15 7 ♐ 00R	1/10 27 ♐ 00	10/26 20 ♑ 01
8/ 9 3 ♏ 01	5/ 5 5 ♐ 00R	1/30 0 ♑ 00	11/15 23 ♑ 00
8/29 5 ♏ 00	5/25 3 ♐ 00R	2/19 2 ♑ 00	12/ 5 26 ♑ 01
9/18 7 ♏ 00	6/14 0 ♐ 01R	3/11 3 ♑ 01	12/25 0 ♒ 01
10/ 8 9 ♏ 01	7/ 4 29 ♏ 00R	3/31 4 ♑ 01	2058
10/28 12 ♏ 00	7/24 27 ♏ 01R	4/20 4 ♑ 01R	1/14 4 ♒ 01
11/17 15 ♏ 00	8/13 27 ♏ 01	5/10 3 ♑ 01R	2/ 3 9 ♒ 01
12/ 7 17 ♏ 01	9/ 2 28 ♏ 00	5/30 1 ♑ 01R	2/23 14 ♒ 00
12/27 20 ♏ 00	9/22 29 ♏ 00	6/19 28 ♐ 01R	3/15 18 ♒ 01
2050	10/12 1 ♐ 00	7/ 9 26 ♐ 00R	4/ 4 22 ♒ 01
1/16 22 ♏ 00	11/ 1 3 ♐ 01	7/29 24 ♐ 00R	4/24 26 ♒ 00
2/ 5 23 ♏ 00	11/21 6 ♐ 00	8/18 22 ♐ 01R	5/14 28 ♒ 01
2/25 23 ♏ 01R	12/11 8 ♐ 01	9/ 7 22 ♐ 01	6/ 3 0 ♓ 00
3/17 22 ♏ 01R	12/31 11 ♐ 00	9/27 23 ♐ 00	6/23 0 ♓ 00R
4/ 6 21 ♏ 00R	2053	10/17 24 ♐ 01	7/13 28 ♒ 00R
4/26 19 ♏ 00R	1/20 13 ♐ 00	11/ 6 26 ♐ 01	8/ 2 25 ♒ 00R
5/16 16 ♏ 01R	2/ 9 14 ♐ 01	11/26 29 ♐ 01	8/22 20 ♒ 01R
6/ 5 14 ♏ 01R	3/ 1 16 ♐ 00	12/16 2 ♑ 01	9/11 16 ♒ 01R
6/25 13 ♏ 00R	3/21 16 ♐ 00R	2056	10/ 1 14 ♒ 00R
7/15 12 ♏ 00R	4/10 15 ♐ 01R	1/ 5 6 ♑ 00	10/21 13 ♒ 01
8/ 4 12 ♏ 00	4/30 14 ♐ 00R	1/25 9 ♑ 00	11/10 14 ♒ 01
8/24 13 ♏ 00	5/20 12 ♐ 00R	2/14 12 ♑ 00	11/30 17 ♒ 00
9/13 14 ♏ 01	6/ 9 9 ♐ 01R	3/ 5 14 ♑ 00	12/20 21 ♒ 00
10/ 3 16 ♏ 01	6/29 7 ♐ 01R	3/25 16 ♑ 00	2059
10/23 19 ♏ 00	7/19 6 ♐ 00R	4/14 17 ♑ 00	1/ 9 26 ♒ 00
11/12 21 ♏ 01	8/ 8 5 ♐ 00R	5/ 4 17 ♑ 00R	1/29 1 ♓ 01
12/ 2 24 ♏ 00	8/28 5 ♐ 00	5/24 15 ♑ 01R	2/18 7 ♓ 01
12/22 26 ♏ 01	9/17 6 ♐ 00	6/13 13 ♑ 01R	3/10 13 ♓ 01
2051	10/ 7 7 ♐ 01	7/ 3 10 ♑ 01R	3/30 20 ♓ 00
1/11 28 ♏ 01	10/27 9 ♐ 01	7/23 7 ♑ 01R	4/19 26 ♓ 00
1/31 0 ♐ 00	11/16 12 ♐ 00	8/12 5 ♑ 01R	5/ 9 2 ♈ 01
2/20 1 ♐ 00	12/ 6 14 ♐ 01	9/ 1 4 ♑ 00R	5/29 8 ♈ 00
3/12 1 ♐ 00R	12/26 17 ♐ 01	9/21 4 ♑ 00	6/18 13 ♈ 00
4/ 1 0 ♐ 00R	2054	10/11 5 ♑ 00	7/ 8 17 ♈ 01
4/21 28 ♏ 01R	1/15 20 ♐ 00	10/31 6 ♑ 01	7/28 20 ♈ 00
5/11 26 ♏ 00R	2/ 4 22 ♐ 01	11/20 9 ♑ 01	8/17 21 ♈ 00R
5/31 24 ♏ 00R	2/24 23 ♐ 01	12/10 12 ♑ 01	9/ 6 19 ♈ 01R
6/20 22 ♏ 00R	3/16 24 ♐ 01	12/30 16 ♑ 01	9/26 15 ♈ 01R
7/10 20 ♏ 01R	4/ 5 24 ♐ 01R	2057	10/16 9 ♈ 01R
7/30 20 ♏ 00R	4/25 23 ♐ 01R	1/19 20 ♑ 00	11/ 5 4 ♈ 01R
8/19 20 ♏ 01	5/15 22 ♐ 00R	2/ 8 24 ♑ 00	11/25 2 ♈ 00R
9/ 8 21 ♏ 01	6/ 4 19 ♐ 01R	2/28 27 ♑ 01	12/15 2 ♈ 01

2060	9/30 29 ♎ 01	6/26 22 ♏ 00R	3/22 25 ♐ 00
1/ 4 6 ♈ 01	10/20 3 ♏ 00	7/16 21 ♏ 00R	4/11 24 ♐ 01R
1/24 12 ♈ 01	11/ 9 6 ♏ 00	8/ 5 20 ♏ 01	5/ 1 23 ♐ 01R
2/13 21 ♈ 00	11/29 9 ♏ 00	8/25 21 ♏ 00	5/21 21 ♐ 01R
3/ 4 0 ♉ 01	12/19 11 ♏ 01	9/14 22 ♏ 00	6/10 19 ♐ 01R
3/24 11 ♉ 01	2063	10/ 4 24 ♏ 00	6/30 17 ♐ 00R
4/13 24 ♉ 00	1/ 8 13 ♏ 01	10/24 26 ♏ 00	7/20 15 ♐ 00R
5/ 3 7 ♊ 01	1/28 15 ♏ 00	11/13 28 ♏ 01	8/ 9 13 ♐ 01R
5/23 21 ♊ 01	2/17 15 ♏ 01R	12/ 3 1 ♐ 00	8/29 13 ♐ 01
6/12 6 ♋ 00	3/ 9 15 ♏ 00R	12/23 3 ♐ 01	9/18 14 ♐ 00
7/ 2 20 ♋ 00	3/29 13 ♏ 00R	2066	10/ 8 15 ♐ 01
7/22 4 ♌ 00	4/18 11 ♏ 00R	1/12 5 ♐ 01	10/28 17 ♐ 01
8/11 16 ♌ 01	5/ 8 8 ♏ 01R	2/ 1 7 ♐ 01	11/17 20 ♐ 00
8/31 28 ♌ 01	5/28 6 ♏ 00R	2/21 8 ♐ 01	12/ 7 23 ♐ 00
9/20 8 ♍ 01	6/17 4 ♏ 00R	3/13 9 ♐ 00R	12/27 25 ♐ 01
10/10 18 ♍ 00	7/ 7 3 ♏ 01R	4/ 2 8 ♐ 00R	2069
10/30 26 ♍ 01	7/27 3 ♏ 01	4/22 7 ♐ 00R	1/16 28 ♐ 01
11/19 3 ♎ 00	8/16 4 ♏ 01	5/12 5 ♐ 00R	2/ 5 1 ♑ 00
12/ 9 8 ♎ 01	9/ 5 6 ♏ 00	6/ 1 2 ♐ 01R	2/25 3 ♑ 00
12/29 12 ♎ 00	9/25 8 ♏ 01	6/21 0 ♐ 01R	3/17 4 ♑ 01
2061	10/15 11 ♏ 00	7/11 29 ♏ 00R	4/ 6 5 ♑ 00
1/18 13 ♎ 01	11/ 4 13 ♏ 01	7/31 28 ♏ 00R	4/26 4 ♑ 01R
2/ 7 12 ♎ 01R	11/24 16 ♏ 01	8/20 28 ♏ 00	5/16 3 ♑ 00R
2/27 9 ♎ 00R	12/14 19 ♏ 00	9/ 9 29 ♏ 00	6/ 5 1 ♑ 00R
3/19 4 ♎ 00R	2064	9/29 0 ♐ 00	6/25 28 ♐ 01R
4/ 8 29 ♍ 01R	1/ 3 21 ♏ 00	10/19 2 ♐ 00	7/15 26 ♐ 00R
4/28 26 ♍ 01R	1/23 23 ♏ 00	11/ 8 4 ♐ 01	8/ 4 24 ♐ 00R
5/18 25 ♍ 01R	2/12 23 ♏ 01	11/28 7 ♐ 00	8/24 23 ♐ 00R
6/ 7 26 ♍ 00	3/ 3 24 ♏ 00R	12/18 9 ♐ 01	9/13 23 ♐ 00
6/27 27 ♍ 01	3/23 23 ♏ 00R	2067	10/ 3 24 ♐ 00
7/17 0 ♎ 01	4/12 21 ♏ 00R	1/ 7 12 ♐ 00	10/23 25 ♐ 01
8/ 6 4 ♎ 01	5/ 2 19 ♏ 00R	1/27 14 ♐ 00	11/12 28 ♐ 00
8/26 8 ♎ 01	5/22 16 ♏ 01R	2/16 15 ♐ 01	12/ 2 1 ♑ 00
9/15 12 ♎ 01	6/11 14 ♏ 01R	3/ 8 16 ♐ 01	12/22 4 ♑ 00
10/ 5 17 ♎ 00	7/ 1 13 ♏ 00R	3/28 16 ♐ 01R	2070
10/25 21 ♎ 01	7/21 12 ♏ 01R	4/17 15 ♐ 01R	1/11 7 ♑ 01
11/14 25 ♎ 01	8/10 13 ♏ 00	5/ 7 14 ♐ 00R	1/31 10 ♑ 01
12/ 4 29 ♎ 00	8/30 14 ♏ 00	5/27 11 ♐ 01R	2/20 13 ♑ 00
12/24 2 ♏ 00	9/19 15 ♏ 01	6/16 9 ♐ 01R	3/12 15 ♑ 01
2062	10/ 9 17 ♏ 01	7/ 6 7 ♐ 01R	4/ 1 17 ♑ 00
1/13 3 ♏ 01	10/29 20 ♏ 00	7/26 6 ♐ 00R	4/21 17 ♑ 01
2/ 2 4 ♏ 01	11/18 23 ♏ 00	8/15 5 ♐ 01R	5/11 17 ♑ 00R
2/22 4 ♏ 00R	12/ 8 25 ♏ 01	9/ 4 5 ♐ 01	5/31 15 ♑ 01R
3/14 2 ♏ 01R	12/28 27 ♏ 01	9/24 6 ♐ 01	6/20 13 ♑ 00R
4/ 3 29 ♎ 01R	2065	10/14 8 ♐ 01	7/10 10 ♑ 00R
4/23 26 ♎ 01R	1/17 29 ♏ 01	11/ 3 10 ♐ 01	7/30 7 ♑ 01R
5/13 23 ♎ 01R	2/ 6 1 ♐ 00	11/23 13 ♐ 00	8/19 5 ♑ 00R
6/ 2 21 ♎ 01R	2/26 1 ♐ 01	12/13 16 ♐ 00	9/ 8 4 ♑ 01R
6/22 20 ♎ 01R	3/18 1 ♐ 00R	2068	9/28 4 ♑ 01
7/12 21 ♎ 00	4/ 7 0 ♐ 00R	1/ 2 18 ♐ 01	10/18 6 ♑ 00
8/ 1 22 ♎ 00	4/27 28 ♏ 00R	1/22 21 ♐ 00	11/ 7 8 ♑ 00
8/21 24 ♎ 00	5/17 26 ♏ 00R	2/11 23 ♐ 00	11/27 11 ♑ 00
9/10 27 ♎ 00	6/ 6 23 ♏ 01R	3/ 2 24 ♐ 01	12/17 14 ♑ 01

2071	10/ 2 19 ♈ 00R	6/28 21 ♎ 01R	3/25 1 ♐ 01R
1/ 6 18 ♑ 00	10/22 13 ♈ 00R	7/18 22 ♎ 01	4/14 0 ♐ 00R
1/26 22 ♑ 00	11/11 8 ♈ 00R	8/ 7 23 ♎ 01	5/ 4 28 ♏ 00R
2/15 25 ♑ 01	12/ 1 6 ♈ 00R	8/27 26 ♎ 00	5/24 26 ♏ 00R
3/ 7 29 ♑ 00	12/21 7 ♈ 00	9/16 28 ♎ 01	6/13 23 ♏ 01R
3/27 2 ♒ 00	2074	10/ 6 1 ♏ 01	7/ 3 22 ♏ 00R
4/16 4 ♒ 00	1/10 11 ♈ 01	10/26 4 ♏ 01	7/23 21 ♏ 00R
5/ 6 5 ♒ 00	1/30 18 ♈ 01	11/15 7 ♏ 01	8/12 21 ♏ 00
5/26 4 ♒ 01R	2/19 27 ♈ 01	12/ 5 10 ♏ 01	9/ 1 22 ♏ 00
6/15 3 ♒ 00R	3/11 8 ♉ 01	12/25 13 ♏ 00	9/21 23 ♏ 00
7/ 5 0 ♒ 01R	3/31 20 ♉ 01	2077	10/11 25 ♏ 00
7/25 27 ♑ 00R	4/20 4 ♊ 00	1/14 15 ♏ 00	10/31 27 ♏ 01
8/14 23 ♑ 01R	5/10 18 ♊ 00	2/ 3 16 ♏ 00	11/20 0 ♐ 00
9/ 3 21 ♑ 00R	5/30 2 ♋ 01	2/23 16 ♏ 00R	12/10 2 ♐ 01
9/23 20 ♑ 00R	6/19 16 ♋ 01	3/15 15 ♏ 00R	12/30 5 ♐ 00
10/13 20 ♑ 01	7/ 9 0 ♌ 01	4/ 4 13 ♏ 01R	2080
11/ 2 22 ♑ 00	7/29 13 ♌ 00	4/24 11 ♏ 00R	1/19 7 ♐ 00
11/22 24 ♑ 01	8/18 25 ♌ 00	5/14 8 ♏ 00R	2/ 8 8 ♐ 01
12/12 28 ♑ 01	9/ 7 5 ♍ 01	6/ 3 6 ♏ 00R	2/28 9 ♐ 01
2072	9/27 15 ♍ 00	6/23 4 ♏ 01R	3/19 9 ♐ 01R
1/ 1 2 ♒ 01	10/17 24 ♍ 00	7/13 4 ♏ 00R	4/ 8 8 ♐ 01R
1/21 7 ♒ 00	11/ 6 1 ♎ 00	8/ 2 4 ♏ 01	4/28 7 ♐ 00R
2/10 11 ♒ 01	11/26 7 ♎ 01	8/22 5 ♏ 01	5/18 4 ♐ 01R
3/ 1 16 ♒ 01	12/16 12 ♎ 00	9/11 7 ♏ 01	6/ 7 2 ♐ 01R
3/21 20 ♒ 01	2075	10/ 1 10 ♏ 00	6/27 0 ♐ 01R
4/10 24 ♒ 01	1/ 5 15 ♎ 00	10/21 12 ♏ 01	7/17 29 ♏ 00R
4/30 28 ♒ 00	1/25 15 ♎ 01R	11/10 15 ♏ 00	8/ 6 28 ♏ 01R
5/20 0 ♓ 01	2/14 14 ♎ 00R	11/30 18 ♏ 00	8/26 28 ♏ 01
6/ 9 1 ♓ 01	3/ 6 10 ♎ 01R	12/20 20 ♏ 01	9/15 29 ♏ 01
6/29 1 ♓ 00R	3/26 5 ♎ 01R	2078	10/ 5 1 ♐ 01
7/19 29 ♒ 00R	4/15 1 ♎ 01R	1/ 9 22 ♏ 00	10/25 3 ♐ 01
8/ 8 25 ♒ 00R	5/ 5 28 ♍ 01R	1/29 24 ♏ 00	11/14 6 ♐ 00
8/28 21 ♒ 00R	5/25 27 ♍ 01R	2/18 24 ♏ 01	12/ 4 8 ♐ 01
9/17 17 ♒ 00R	6/14 28 ♍ 01	3/10 24 ♏ 00R	12/24 11 ♐ 00
10/ 7 15 ♒ 00R	7/ 4 0 ♎ 01	3/30 23 ♏ 00R	2081
10/27 15 ♒ 00	7/24 3 ♎ 01	4/19 21 ♏ 00R	1/13 13 ♐ 01
11/16 16 ♒ 01	8/13 7 ♎ 00	5/ 9 19 ♏ 00R	2/ 2 15 ♐ 01
12/ 6 19 ♒ 01	9/ 2 11 ♎ 00	5/29 16 ♏ 01R	2/22 16 ♐ 01
12/26 24 ♒ 00	9/22 15 ♎ 01	6/18 14 ♏ 01R	3/14 17 ♐ 01
2073	10/12 19 ♎ 01	7/ 8 13 ♏ 01R	4/ 3 17 ♐ 00R
1/15 29 ♒ 00	11/ 1 24 ♎ 00	7/28 13 ♏ 00	4/23 16 ♐ 00R
2/ 4 4 ♓ 01	11/21 27 ♎ 01	8/17 13 ♏ 01	5/13 14 ♐ 00R
2/24 11 ♓ 00	12/11 1 ♏ 00	9/ 6 15 ♏ 00	6/ 2 11 ♐ 01R
3/16 17 ♓ 00	12/31 3 ♏ 01	9/26 16 ♏ 01	6/22 9 ♐ 01R
4/ 5 23 ♓ 01	2076	10/16 19 ♏ 00	7/12 7 ♐ 01R
4/25 0 ♈ 00	1/20 5 ♏ 00	11/ 5 21 ♏ 00	8/ 1 6 ♐ 01R
5/15 6 ♈ 01	2/ 9 5 ♏ 01R	11/25 24 ♏ 00	8/21 6 ♐ 00
6/ 4 12 ♈ 00	2/29 4 ♏ 01R	12/15 26 ♏ 01	9/10 6 ♐ 01
6/24 17 ♈ 01	3/20 2 ♏ 01R	2079	9/30 8 ♐ 00
7/14 21 ♈ 01	4/ 9 29 ♎ 01R	1/ 4 29 ♏ 00	10/20 9 ♐ 01
8/ 3 24 ♈ 01	4/29 26 ♎ 01R	1/24 0 ♐ 01	11/ 9 12 ♐ 00
8/23 25 ♈ 01R	5/19 24 ♎ 00R	2/13 1 ♐ 01	11/29 15 ♐ 00
9/12 23 ♈ 01R	6/ 8 22 ♎ 01R	3/ 5 2 ♐ 00R	12/19 17 ♐ 01

Hidalgo Tables

2082	10/ 4 7 ♑ 00	7/ 1 11 ♉ 00	3/27 7 ♏ 00R
1/ 8 20 ♐ 00	10/24 8 ♑ 01	7/21 19 ♉ 00	4/16 4 ♏ 01R
1/28 22 ♐ 01	11/13 11 ♑ 00	8/10 27 ♉ 00	5/ 6 1 ♏ 01R
2/17 24 ♐ 01	12/ 3 14 ♑ 01	8/30 5 ♊ 00	5/26 29 ♎ 00R
3/ 9 25 ♐ 01	12/23 18 ♑ 00	9/19 12 ♊ 01	6/15 27 ♎ 01R
3/29 26 ♐ 00R	2085	10/ 9 19 ♊ 00	7/ 5 27 ♎ 00R
4/18 25 ♐ 01R	1/12 22 ♑ 00	10/29 23 ♊ 01	7/25 27 ♎ 01
5/ 8 24 ♐ 00R	2/ 1 26 ♑ 00	11/18 25 ♊ 00R	8/14 28 ♎ 01
5/28 22 ♐ 00R	2/21 0 ♒ 00	12/ 8 22 ♊ 00R	9/ 3 0 ♏ 01
6/17 19 ♐ 01R	3/13 3 ♒ 01	12/28 16 ♊ 01R	9/23 3 ♏ 00
7/ 7 17 ♐ 00R	4/ 2 6 ♒ 01	2088	10/13 6 ♏ 00
7/27 15 ♐ 01R	4/22 8 ♒ 01	1/17 15 ♊ 01	11/ 2 9 ♏ 00
8/16 14 ♐ 01R	5/12 10 ♒ 00	2/ 6 19 ♊ 01	11/22 12 ♏ 00
9/ 5 14 ♐ 01	6/ 1 9 ♒ 01R	2/26 28 ♊ 00	12/12 14 ♏ 01
9/25 15 ♐ 00	6/21 8 ♒ 00R	3/17 8 ♋ 00	2091
10/15 17 ♐ 00	7/11 5 ♒ 00R	4/ 6 18 ♋ 00	1/ 1 17 ♏ 00
11/ 4 19 ♐ 00	7/31 1 ♒ 00R	4/26 28 ♋ 00	1/21 18 ♏ 01
11/24 22 ♐ 00	8/20 27 ♑ 01R	5/16 8 ♌ 00	2/10 19 ♏ 01
12/14 25 ♐ 00	9/ 9 25 ♑ 00R	6/ 5 17 ♌ 00	3/ 2 19 ♏ 01R
2083	9/29 24 ♑ 00R	6/25 25 ♌ 01	3/22 18 ♏ 01R
1/ 3 27 ♐ 01	10/19 25 ♑ 00	7/15 4 ♍ 00	4/11 16 ♏ 01R
1/23 0 ♑ 01	11/ 8 26 ♑ 01	8/ 4 12 ♍ 00	5/ 1 14 ♏ 00R
2/12 3 ♑ 00	11/28 0 ♒ 00	8/24 19 ♍ 01	5/21 11 ♏ 01R
3/ 4 5 ♑ 00	12/18 4 ♒ 00	9/13 26 ♍ 01	6/10 9 ♏ 01R
3/24 6 ♑ 01	2086	10/ 3 3 ♎ 00	6/30 8 ♏ 00R
4/13 6 ♑ 01R	1/ 7 8 ♒ 01	10/23 9 ♎ 00	7/20 8 ♏ 00
5/ 3 6 ♑ 00R	1/27 13 ♒ 01	11/12 14 ♎ 01	8/ 9 8 ♏ 00
5/23 4 ♑ 01R	2/16 18 ♒ 01	12/ 2 19 ♎ 00	8/29 9 ♏ 01
6/12 2 ♑ 00R	3/ 8 23 ♒ 01	12/22 22 ♎ 01	9/18 11 ♏ 01
7/ 2 29 ♐ 00R	3/28 28 ♒ 01	2089	10/ 8 13 ♏ 01
7/22 26 ♐ 01R	4/17 3 ♓ 00	1/11 24 ♎ 01	10/28 16 ♏ 00
8/11 25 ♐ 00R	5/ 7 7 ♓ 00	1/31 25 ♎ 00R	11/17 19 ♏ 00
8/31 24 ♐ 00R	5/27 10 ♓ 00	2/20 24 ♎ 00R	12/ 7 21 ♏ 01
9/20 24 ♐ 01	6/16 12 ♓ 00	3/12 21 ♎ 00R	12/27 24 ♏ 00
10/10 25 ♐ 01	7/ 6 12 ♓ 00R	4/ 1 17 ♎ 01R	2092
10/30 27 ♐ 01	7/26 10 ♓ 00R	4/21 13 ♎ 01R	1/16 25 ♏ 01
11/19 0 ♑ 00	8/15 6 ♓ 00R	5/11 11 ♎ 00R	2/ 5 27 ♏ 00
12/ 9 3 ♑ 01	9/ 4 1 ♓ 01R	5/31 9 ♎ 01R	2/25 27 ♏ 01
12/29 6 ♑ 01	9/24 27 ♒ 00R	6/20 9 ♎ 00	3/16 27 ♏ 00R
2084	10/14 24 ♒ 01R	7/10 10 ♎ 01	4/ 5 26 ♏ 00R
1/18 10 ♑ 00	11/ 3 24 ♒ 00	7/30 12 ♎ 01	4/25 24 ♏ 00R
2/ 7 13 ♑ 01	11/23 26 ♒ 00	8/19 15 ♎ 01	5/15 21 ♏ 01R
2/27 16 ♑ 00	12/13 29 ♒ 01	9/ 8 19 ♎ 00	6/ 4 19 ♏ 01R
3/18 18 ♑ 01	2087	9/28 22 ♎ 01	6/24 17 ♏ 01R
4/ 7 20 ♑ 00	1/ 2 4 ♓ 00	10/18 26 ♎ 00	7/14 16 ♏ 01R
4/27 20 ♑ 01R	1/22 10 ♓ 00	11/ 7 0 ♏ 00	8/ 3 16 ♏ 01
5/17 19 ♑ 01R	2/11 16 ♓ 01	11/27 3 ♏ 00	8/23 17 ♏ 00
6/ 6 18 ♑ 00R	3/ 3 23 ♓ 01	12/17 6 ♏ 00	9/12 18 ♏ 01
6/26 15 ♑ 00R	3/23 1 ♈ 00	2090	10/ 2 20 ♏ 00
7/16 12 ♑ 00R	4/12 8 ♈ 01	1/ 6 8 ♏ 01	10/22 22 ♏ 01
8/ 5 9 ♑ 00R	5/ 2 16 ♈ 01	1/26 9 ♏ 01	11/11 25 ♏ 00
8/25 7 ♑ 00R	5/22 24 ♈ 01	2/15 10 ♏ 00R	12/ 1 27 ♏ 01
9/14 6 ♑ 01R	6/11 2 ♉ 01	3/ 7 9 ♏ 00R	12/21 0 ♐ 00

2093	10/ 7 11 ♐ 01	7/ 3 21 ♑ 00R
1/10 2 ♐ 00	10/27 13 ♐ 01	7/23 17 ♑ 01R
1/30 3 ♐ 01	11/16 16 ♐ 00	8/12 14 ♑ 01R
2/19 4 ♐ 01	12/ 6 18 ♐ 01	9/ 1 12 ♑ 01R
3/11 5 ♐ 00R	12/26 21 ♐ 01	9/21 12 ♑ 00
3/31 4 ♐ 00R	2096	10/11 12 ♑ 01
4/20 2 ♐ 01R	1/15 24 ♐ 00	10/31 14 ♑ 01
5/10 0 ♐ 01R	2/ 4 26 ♐ 01	11/20 17 ♑ 01
5/30 28 ♏ 01R	2/24 28 ♐ 01	12/10 21 ♑ 00
6/19 26 ♏ 01R	3/15 29 ♐ 01	12/30 24 ♑ 01
7/ 9 25 ♏ 00R	4/ 4 0 ♑ 00R	2099
7/29 24 ♏ 00R	4/24 29 ♐ 01R	1/19 29 ♑ 00
8/18 24 ♏ 00	5/14 27 ♐ 01R	2/ 8 3 ♒ 01
9/ 7 25 ♏ 00	6/ 3 25 ♐ 01R	2/28 7 ♒ 01
9/27 26 ♏ 01	6/23 23 ♐ 00R	3/20 11 ♒ 01
10/17 28 ♏ 01	7/13 20 ♐ 01R	4/ 9 15 ♒ 00
11/ 6 1 ♐ 00	8/ 2 18 ♐ 01R	4/29 17 ♒ 01
11/26 3 ♐ 01	8/22 18 ♐ 00R	5/19 19 ♒ 00
12/16 6 ♐ 00	9/11 18 ♐ 00	6/ 8 19 ♒ 00R
2094	10/ 1 19 ♐ 00	6/28 17 ♒ 01R
1/ 5 8 ♐ 01	10/21 21 ♐ 00	7/18 14 ♒ 01R
1/25 10 ♐ 01	11/10 23 ♐ 00	8/ 7 10 ♒ 01R
2/14 11 ♐ 01	11/30 26 ♐ 00	8/27 6 ♒ 01R
3/ 6 12 ♐ 01	12/20 29 ♐ 00	9/16 4 ♒ 00R
3/26 12 ♐ 01R	2097	10/ 6 2 ♒ 01R
4/15 11 ♐ 01R	1/ 9 2 ♑ 00	10/26 3 ♒ 00
5/ 5 9 ♐ 01R	1/29 5 ♑ 00	11/15 5 ♒ 01
5/25 7 ♐ 01R	2/18 8 ♑ 00	12/ 5 8 ♒ 01
6/14 5 ♐ 00R	3/10 10 ♑ 00	12/25 13 ♒ 00
7/ 4 3 ♐ 00R	3/30 11 ♑ 00	2100
7/24 2 ♐ 00R	4/19 11 ♑ 01R	1/14 18 ♒ 00
8/13 1 ♐ 01R	5/ 9 10 ♑ 01R	2/ 3 23 ♒ 01
9/ 2 1 ♐ 01	5/29 8 ♑ 01R	2/23 29 ♒ 00
9/22 3 ♐ 00	6/18 6 ♑ 00R	3/15 4 ♓ 01
10/12 4 ♐ 01	7/ 8 3 ♑ 00R	4/ 4 10 ♓ 01
11/ 1 7 ♐ 00	7/28 0 ♑ 01R	4/24 15 ♓ 01
11/21 9 ♐ 01	8/17 29 ♐ 00R	5/14 20 ♓ 01
12/11 12 ♐ 00	9/ 6 28 ♐ 00R	6/ 3 24 ♓ 01
12/31 14 ♐ 01	9/26 28 ♐ 01	6/23 27 ♓ 01
2095	10/16 0 ♑ 00	7/13 29 ♓ 00
1/20 17 ♐ 00	11/ 5 2 ♑ 01	8/ 2 28 ♓ 01R
2/ 9 19 ♐ 00	11/25 5 ♑ 00	8/22 25 ♓ 01R
3/ 1 20 ♐ 00	12/15 8 ♑ 01	9/11 21 ♓ 00R
3/21 20 ♐ 01	2098	10/ 1 15 ♓ 01R
4/10 20 ♐ 00R	1/ 4 12 ♑ 00	10/21 12 ♓ 00R
4/30 19 ♐ 00R	1/24 15 ♑ 01	11/10 10 ♓ 01R
5/20 17 ♐ 00R	2/13 19 ♑ 00	11/30 11 ♓ 01
6/ 9 14 ♐ 01R	3/ 5 22 ♑ 00	12/20 15 ♓ 00
6/29 12 ♐ 00R	3/25 24 ♑ 01	
7/19 10 ♐ 01R	4/14 26 ♑ 00	
8/ 8 9 ♐ 01R	5/ 4 26 ♑ 01R	
8/28 9 ♐ 00	5/24 26 ♑ 00R	
9/17 10 ♐ 00	6/13 24 ♑ 00R	

About the Author

Gayle Geffner has been an astrologer for over thirty-five years. She has published articles in the *Aspect Magazine* (USA), The Regulus Ebertin Newsletter (Australia), *Today's Astrologer,* published by the American Federation of Astrologers (USA) and Baltimore, Maryland Chapter of *NCGR Newsletter, NCGR Memberletter* (international) and *NCGR Geocosmic Journal* (international). Gayle is also author of *Astrology for Career Success*, and its earlier version *Pathways to Success: Discover Your Career Potential with Astrology*, both published by ACS Publications, and she is also author of the book, *Creative Step-Parenting*, published by American Federation of Astrologers. She is co-author, with Barbara Hawkins, *Astrology At A Glance: A Guide for Astrological Delineation* published by American Federation of Astrologers, which is a classroom guide.

Gayle's academic degrees include a BA in History from California State University, and two paralegal certificates from University of West Los Angeles School of Law (in corporations and in litigation). She currently lives in Los Angeles, CA.

To contact the author, write to:
Gayle Geffner
c/o ACS Publications, Starcrafts LLC
334-A Calef Highway
Epping, NH 03042

Also from Starcrafts LLC
Imprints: *Starcrafts Publishing, ACS Publications*

All About Astrology, a series of booklets by various authors
The American Atlas, Expanded 5th Edition, Thomas G. Shanks
The American Ephemeris 1950-2050 [at Noon or at Midnight],
Trans-Century Edition, by Neil F. Michelsen and Rique Pottenger
The American Ephemeris for the 21st Century 2000-2050 [at Noon or at Midnight],
Revised & Expanded Third Edition, Neil F. Michelsen and Rique Pottenger
The American Heliocentric Ephemeris 2001-2050, Neil F. Michelsen
The American Sidereal Ephemeris 2001-2025, Neil F. Michelsen
Archetypes of Astrology Ena Stanley
The Asteroid Ephemeris 1900-2050, Rique Pottenger with Neil F. Michelsen
Astrology for Career Success, Gayle Geffner
Astrology for the Light Side of the Brain, Kim Rogers-Gallagher
Astrology for the Light Side of the Future, Kim Rogers-Gallagher
Astrology: the Next Step, Maritha Pottenger
Astrology and Weight Control, Beverly Ann Flynn
The Book of Jupiter, Marilyn Waram   .   *Chocolate Sauce* Pat Geisler
Dial Detective, Revised Second Edition, Maria Kay Simms
Easy Astrology Guide, Maritha Pottenger   .   *Easy Tarot Guide*, Marcia Masino
Future Signs, Maria Kay Simms
The International Atlas, Revised 6th Edition, Thomas G. Shanks & Rique Pottenger
The Michelsen Book of Tables, Neil F. Michelsen
Moon Tides, Soul Passages, Maria Kay Simms, with software CD by Rique Pottenger
The New American Ephemeris for the 20th Century, 1900-2000, at Midnight
Michelsen Memorial Edition, Rique Pottenger, based on Michelsen
The New American Ephemeris for the 20th Century, 1900-2000, at Noon
Michelsen Memorial Edition, Rique Pottenger, based on Michelsen
The New American Ephemeris for the 21st Century, 2000-2100 at Midnight
Michelsen Memorial Edition, Rique Pottenger, based on Michelsen
The New American Ephemeris for the 21st Century, 2007-2020:
Rique Pottenger, based on Michelsen
The New American Midpoint Ephemeris 2007-2020, Rique Pottenger, based on Michelsen
The Only Way to Learn Astrology, Volumes. 1-6 series, Marion D. March & Joan McEvers
Past Lives, Future Choices, Maritha Pottenger   .   *Planetary Heredity*, Michel Gauquelin
Planets on the Move, Maritha Pottenger and Zipporah Dobyns, Ph.D.
The Plain Vanilla Astrologer, Pat Geisler   *Psychology of the Planets*, Francoise Gauquelin
Spirit Guides Iris Belhayes
Tables of Planetary Phenomena, Third Edition, Neil F. Michelsen
Unveiling Your Future, Maritha Pottenger and Zipporah Dobyns, Ph.D.
Yankee Doodle Discord: A Walk with Eris through USA History, Thomas Canfield
Your Magical Child, Maria Kay Simms   .   *Your Starway to Love*, Maritha Pottenger

Now you can order HIDALGO in your Astro Computing Services Charts!

Hidalgo has been added to the list of free "extra bodies" available in our charts. Just ask for Hidalgo when you place a chart order!

The charts illustrated within this book are our **One-Ring Wheel Chart (with aspect lines)**, normally in color..........PNAT $6.95

Pictured below in miniature is Astro's oldest and most popular **BNC chart** (normally a full letter size page, black & white) with extensive listings of data, midpoint, etc. ....BNC $6.95

Astro Keys Information Special– 2 pages list of keywords for signs, planets, aspect & asteroids ane more, Hidalgo..........$,1.00

Asteroid Calculations–a 1 page listing positions of your planets, MC, Asc and 19 asteroids inluding Hidalgo & Chiron..........$7.95

Many Interesting Asteroids– a zodiacal sort in four columns of asteroids, including Hildalgo and Chiron, with two options.

Option 1: A 2 page zodiacal sort by zodiacal order $7.95
Option 2: A 4 page alphabetical sort by name..................$9.95

www.astrocom.com
24-hour toll-free order line: 866-953-8458

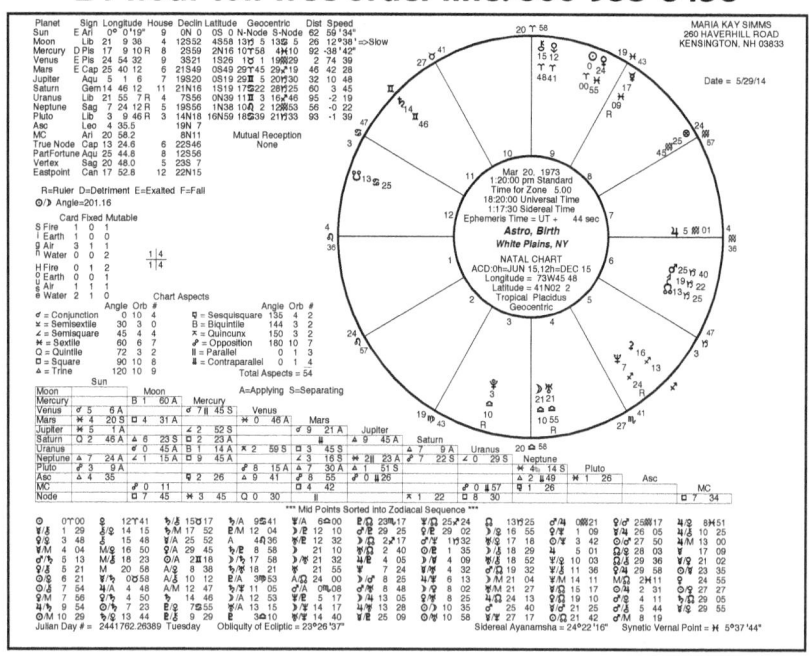

Are you an astrologer whose clients are planning for a career or for making a career change?

Or, are YOU looking for a career change, and understand astrology well enough to use it?

THEN THIS BOOK IS FOR YOU!

$15.95

ASTROLOGY for CAREER SUCCESS
How to Analyze Career Choices and Timing

Gayle Geffner

In Gayle Geffner's 25+ years as astrological consultant, she has specialized in career counseling, so this book is a great "how to" for you, if you also want to learn more about this astrological specialty! You'll learn about Gayle's "at least three charts" method, how to find opportunity for career change or advancement in the horoscope, and how to help your clients approach change positively, even when times might be tough. You'll learn a variety of methods, using one, two and three ring charts, including:

- natal astrology
- transits
- solar & lunar returns
- solar arcs
- midpoints
- 90° dial

Explore new options & timing with astrology!

In this book Gayle brings to you her 25+ yearss as a consulting astrologer, and a wealth of real-world experience in careeer counseling!

Astro Computing Services
ACS Publications, an imprint of Starcrafts LLC
www.astrocom.com

The American Ephemeris Series

All of the standard-setting reference works

by Neil F. Michelsen and Rique Pottenger

are now available in newly updated editions

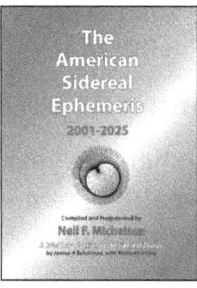

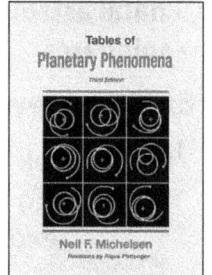

Starcrafts Publishing & ACS Publications
imprints of Starcrafts LLC, 334-A Calef Hwy, Epping, NH 03042
603-734-4300 • www.astrocom.com

Astro's All About Astrology Booklet Series ...

You'll find them to be interesting, helpful and very affordable aids for learning a variety of astrological topics & techniques.

Ardor, Assertion & Anger: Mars in Your Chart 8.95
Ceres in Signs, Houses, Aspects $8.95
The Art of Chart Comparison $4.95
Chiron in Houses, Signs & Aspects $8.95
The East Point & the Antivertex $4.95
  All five above are by Maritha Pottenger
Coalescent Horoscopes $4.95
  Lawrence Grinnel (Dhruva) & David Dukelow
Complete Guide to Establishing a
  Professional Astrological Practice 4.95
  Peggy Larson & Chris Rogers
Eris in Signs, Houses, Aspects $8.95
  Thomas Canfield
History of the Planets Robert Powell $4.95
History of the Houses Robert Powell $4.95
Interpreting Composite & Relationship
  Charts Joan Negus $6.95
Juno: Key to Marriage, Intimacy &
Partnership Maritha Pottenger $6.95
  Maritha Pottenger
Search for the Christmas Star $8.95
  Neil F. Michelsen and Maria Kay Simms
Transpluto $4.95
  David Dukelow and Dhruva
What are Astrolocality Maps? $6.95
  Maritha Pottenger
What Astrology Can Do for You $6.95
  Maritha Pottenger
What are Winning Transits? $5.90
  Joyce Wehrman
Wit & Wisdom: Mercury in your Chart $8.95
  Maritha Pottenger
Your Love Life: Venus in Your Chart $8.95
  Maritha Pottenger
The Zodiac: A Historical Survey Robert Powell $6.95
Zodiac Gift Guide: Gift Ideas for Sun Signs $9.95
  Carol Sandy

Astro Computing Services • Starcrafts LLC
334-A Calef Hwy., Epping, NH 03042 www.astrocom.com

With *The Electronic Astrologer*

You can learn more about astrology, and do charts and reports on your home computer ... it's easy, even for the newest beginner, yet still has the power to please experienced astrologers!

For Windows XP, Vista or 7. Works well on Mac with PC emulator.

With **Reveals Your Horoscope,** you can easily calculate a natal chart for anyone for whom you have birth data.

With **Reveals Your Future**, you have a comprehensive guide to your future based on secondary progressions, transits, eclipses and lunations.

With **Reveals Your Romance**, you can analyze and rate the romantic compatibility of any two individuals. The special score sheet is fun—and revealing—to use!

Print charts & very extensive reports!

Each program —$74.95
Or, buy "all three"—
the *Series* package—for **$175.**

Programmed by Rique Pottenger
Interpreted text by Maritha Pottenger, Zipporah Dobyns and Maria Kay Simms.

includes built in ACS Atlas
See sample reports on our website!

www.astrocom.com
866-953-8458

ACS Publications

Prices subject to change without notice

Come visit Astro Computing Services at www.astrocom.com !

Since founded by Neil F. Michelsen in 1973, Astro has served astrologers worldwide at all levels: beginner, intermediate, professional!

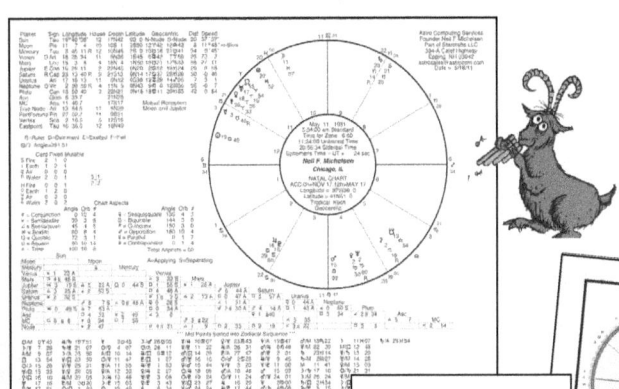

This is still our most popular chart—with more info on one page than any other, & with endless options!

We have lots of other chart styles too, from very complex to clean & easy. Here are two samples of our matted Art Charts, available in five different Astro'toon sets. That's our company chart on the right, with the Ram...

You'll find lots of books to help you learn, a wide variety of interpreted reports ...

... and software, too!

Log on & see what we've got for you!

astrocom.com

www.ingramcontent.com/pod-product-compliance
Lightning Source LLC
Chambersburg PA
CBHW070649050426
42451CB00008B/316